THE
NOWHERE
OFFICE

Also by Julia Hobsbawm

Where the Truth Lies
The See-Saw
Fully Connected
The Simplicity Principle

THE NOWHERE OFFICE

*Reinventing Work and
the Workplace of the Future*

JULIA HOBSBAWM

PUBLICAFFAIRS
New York

To my children who recently entered the world of work and
to my grandson who just entered the world.

———————

PublicAffairs
Hachette Book Group
1290 Avenue of the Americas, New York, NY 10104
www.publicaffairsbooks.com
@Public_Affairs

Printed in the United States of America

Originally published in Great Britain in 2022 by Basic Books London,
an imprint of John Murray Press, an Hachette UK company
First US Edition: April 2022

Published by PublicAffairs, an imprint of Perseus Books, LLC,
a subsidiary of Hachette Book Group, Inc. The PublicAffairs
name and logo is a trademark of the Hachette Book Group.

The Hachette Speakers Bureau provides a wide range of
authors for speaking events. To find out more, go to
www.hachettespeakersbureau.com or call (866) 376-6591.

The publisher is not responsible for websites (or their content)
that are not owned by the publisher.

Library of Congress Control Number: 2021953006

ISBNs: 9781541701939 (hardcover), 9781541701946 (e-book)

LSC-C

Printing 1, 2022

Contents

Preface

Office centricity is over.
Tobi Lütke, CEO Shopify, on Twitter[1]

Imagine you are holding a snow globe in your hand and the object inside is not a place you have been to on holiday or a festive bauble but a representation of where you work. What does it show? Your home? A laptop? A driverless car? For the professional class (which in advanced economies makes up over 40 per cent of the workforce) there is no single obvious image to encapsulate working life any more.[2] Thanks to the internet and automation it could be a smartphone or it could be a makeshift desk under a tree.

It is unlikely to be – at least full time – an actual office. At the centre of work's new snow globe is not a place but a person, whose working life is being shaken up more than at any point in the last hundred years. The Nowhere Office reflects the impact of shifting tectonic plates which were grinding away before Covid-19 happened: technology and its relationship to humans, flexible working – what we now call 'hybrid working' – but also bigger philosophical arguments about the meaning of work itself. As the legendary American social historian Studs Terkel put it in his epic study *Working*: 'Work is about a search for daily meaning as well as daily bread, for recognition as well as cash, for astonishment rather than torpor; in short, for a sort of life rather than a Monday through Friday sort of dying.'[3]

The world of work was already quite sick before the coronavirus took hold. According to the American Institute of Stress 83 per cent of American workers suffer from work-related illnesses. In South Korea the working week was reduced in 2018 because of 'Gwarosa' or 'death from overwork'. The World Health Organisation (WHO) estimates that depression and anxiety alone cost the global economy $1 trillion every year.[4]

The pandemic lifted the lid on a desire to work differently, or less, or with more work–life balance. We can see the impact of this in every metric around work: from 'The Great Resignation' in which millions of American workers resigned en masse and the one in four workers who now imagine they might quit or switch jobs,[5] to the reduction in corporate property rents by as much as 10 per cent with huge changes in the use of office space, co-working space and fixed-lease space.[6] The city has a new competitor: the suburb. This comes as no surprise with the McKinsey Global Institute estimating that up to a quarter of workers in advanced economies will work permanently on a hybrid basis, i.e. partly from home, several days a week.[7] Truly we are nowhere near where we used to be in the middle of Nowhere.

Wherever we end up, working life has been due for a shake-up for a long time. This book attempts to see through the snow blizzard of changes engulfing the world of professional work and to imagine positive changes that could be made to improve it as the post-pandemic world begins to settle.[8]

The Nowhere Office is office life but without the formal fixtures and fittings we took for granted before the pandemic.

It sees a role for the office, but a very changed one. Instead of a single fixed place or schedule, it envisages a mobile, hybrid world which uses HQ offices wisely for certain functions and not for others. It is a new era in professional work which blows away the cobwebs of a stale working model of management and presenteeism and replaces it with a fairer and more functional system that works not only from the top down but also across an organisation.

Snow globes have been around for roughly as long as modern office life (about a hundred years) and while there have been some changes, from glass to plastic, from water to glycerine, from metal shavings to soap flakes, the fundamentals – object, snow, transparent case – remain. Their enduring popularity is simple. They connect us emotionally to two things: the fixed permanence of something we want to keep and the fluttering flash of change and disruption. Humans love both certainty and distraction. The movement of the beautiful flakes swirling around transfixes us but we also like to know where we stand. In the end the snow globe always settles back, but this time the base itself has shifted. This moment is therefore both exciting and uncomfortable. The Nowhere Office represents the moment when those professionals working in business and organisations – the teacher, the technician, the PA, the CEO, the executive in HR, the consultant, the IT expert, the employee, the employer, the freelancer – realise that something fundamental has shifted and that their own snow globe can be reset. That work has been stuck and that change is needed.

The Nowhere Office is a new beginning in the story of the office – if we choose to make it so.

Introduction

Aftermath: the period immediately following a usually ruinous event.

Merriam-Webster dictionary definition

Change is neither good nor bad, it simply is. It can be greeted with terror or joy, a tantrum that says 'I want it the way it was', or a dance that says 'Look, something new'.

Don Draper (*Mad Men*, Season 3, Episode 2)

The office is a byword for modern work. There are 3.3 billion people working in the world,[1] and while the majority still work outside in the fields or in factories, the service sector of knowledge-based work is the fastest growing.[2] The office has come to symbolise what so many of us do for a living, in the way the mill or the assembly line used to. In the Nowhere Office,[3] a new phase of work in which half the professional and technical workforce have the potential to become fully remote-based – and half of workers globally declared that they would quit their jobs if not provided with flexibility – the degree of agency to choose your place and hours of work will come to define us far more than the old classifications.[4] Being labelled a 'white collar' or a 'blue collar' worker could be replaced by being a 'hybrid have' or 'hybrid have-not' worker instead.

The office has captured our imagination in popular culture and in debates about the future of work. When the pandemic locked us out from our workplaces nostalgia grew for TV shows where the star was in many ways the office itself. Viewing figures rocketed. In Amazon Prime's *Bosch*, the gritty LA detective Harry Bosch is frequently shown with his colleagues handling toxic office politics alongside close-ups of cubicle life. Watching Harry do his paperwork is a crucial part of the show. Netflix's comedy drama *Call My Agent!* is also set in an office with lots of people bustling around having showdowns in reception. From *Mad Men* to *The Office*, we seem to enjoy keeping the world of work and its dysfunctions at a safe, entertaining distance. The question of whether people wanted to rush back to the office with the old nine-to-five routine once the pandemic started to subside – something employers and governments were counting on – was clearly more nuanced. People are now asking searching questions about the nature of work, and its meaning to them. In particular they ask what is the point of the office? To work or to socialise? To brainstorm or learn? Or is it really a kind of measuring stick from times gone by, dedicated to presenteeism?

In autumn 2021, I posted a comic Belgian video on Twitter featuring a young girl taking her father 'back to the office' in a charming role reversal showing the kind of anxiety and reluctance familiar to any parent cajoling a child back to school. It went viral, garnering hundreds of thousands of retweets and was seen nearly three million times. 'I've been back in my office for two weeks and this is more accurate than I care to admit', wrote @kelbayar, a programme co-ordinator for the United Nations.

What has happened to so dramatically shift the collective psyche of the world's office workers? This book attempts to answer that question. It isn't as if the philosophical questions about work were not being asked before Covid-19 but they were in the background. The total shutdown of the world's offices focused minds, not least on how much separation there actually is between who we are as human beings and who we are as worker beings.

We've known for years that work was not working properly. It has excluded some people from fair or equal pay, and gender, race or sexual identity equality. And it has locked others into the wrong systems and structures, ensuring failure. The relentless rise of automation and new technologies has kept office life stuck in an endless reboot where instead of using the technology we have, we create new systems and waste time getting used to them. For all the new emphasis on 'well-being' at work it has been neither well nor functional. Stagnant productivity and endemic stress are testament to this.

But more than this the professional and managerial class is now rebelling against the narrative that upward mobility and ever-increasing job responsibility and workload, matched by increasing pay, perks and job titles, are just rewards. Perhaps without the pandemic the busy merry-go-round of the 'always on' life would have continued unabated. There would have been grumbles and some changes but not a wholesale realignment of priorities. But so much changed for so many during the lockdowns. In the Nowhere Office professional work is now challenged by the very people it provides income for, whose loyalty managers and employers used to be able to depend on.[5] They had the upper hand for so long it appears they did not anticipate it would ever change.

This book is not advocating or envisaging a working world denuded of offices but instead reimagines how it can be done better, regardless of location, and possibly in spite of it. The pandemic brought workplaces centre-stage in the debate about the future of work, but the metaphorical place work plays in

3

our lives and the shifts around it should concern us too. No one believes we will have to stop work any time soon or that everyone can and should work from home continuously. The Nowhere Office is a reality check about the moment we are in and an optimistic take on the possibilities afforded by the flux of this moment. We are, in terms of the old fundamentals of fixed working patterns, literally nowhere.[6] The hybrid patterns being introduced today are far from fixed or settled. What matters is where things end up – and that they do so in a way which acknowledges changes that have been building up for decades waiting, perhaps, for this extraordinary time.

The Four Phases of Work

This book is not a history of the office, although the context of how we've moved from a series of localised workforces to sprawling interconnected global hubs linked by certain norms, standards and tech is important. The lunch hour, paternity leave, the office karaoke, after-work drinks – all of these office norms have evolved in fascinating anthropological eddies and flurries along the way. 'You're on mute' is one new addition to the culture and lexicon of work in a constantly updating 'new normal'.

But this book does locate the Nowhere Office as the latest phase in the history of modern work beginning at the end of the Second World War. Why? Because it was a similarly huge moment of social and institutional transition in which the world had to reimagine itself almost wholly after a global event.

I identify four phases of work, the first of which I call the *Optimism Years*, running between 1945 and 1977. In this period faith in corporate institutions and government ran high and was fresh. Technology arrived in the places where work was done, adding both optimism and a futuristic vision of what was to come. The optimism reflected a post-war world rebuilding global institutions and commerce. For instance, market values of commercial property increased from £74 million in 1956 to £395 million by 1970.[7] The Optimism Years represents the blooming of a love affair with corporate real estate which has seen the global market reach $3.9 trillion by 2021.[8] Office buildings rose beyond the imaginations of those who constructed the early skyscrapers of the 1920s and 1930s, beautifully characterised by the Chicago poet Carl Sandburg:

> *It is the men and women, boys and girls so poured in and out all day that give the building a soul of dreams and thoughts and memories.*[9]

After the end of the Second World War, as the world imagined a limitless future, working in skyscrapers felt emotional, important, an optimistic dream. Everyone wanted growth and how better to epitomise it than by looking skywards? The era was captured in the hit TV series *Mad Men*, about the world of advertising, which came into its own during these years. It also captured the endemic sexism of a time when women played a distinctly supporting role to men at work and inequality affected all but white men at the top. The optimism was a combination of wilful blindness, ignorance, and only lasted as long as it did because of economic stability: there were ten times fewer economic crises between 1945 and 1971 compared with the period 1973 to 1997.[10] People were optimistic about society but they were also optimistic about the office: there was no real alternative for the professions. The financial and emotional investment we have made in offices tracks back to the Optimism Years.

The next phase is the *Mezzanine Years*, running between 1978 and 2006, and it represents an intermediate phase for two reasons. First, office work began to feel less like a glamorous luxury and more like a grind and, secondly, technology came into everyone's lives completely with the birth of the internet and the arrival of social media. The office began to feel slightly less perfect or permanent. The phase is named after the ground-breaking 1986 novel by Nicholson Baker, *The Mezzanine*, which takes place almost entirely on the escalators of a gigantic office building and where the protagonist muses philosophically on such matters as whether 'a lunch hour is defined as beginning just as you enter the men's room on the way to lunch, or just as you exit it?'[11] The 1980s and 1990s saw two big shifts: the question of flexibility in the workplace and the phrase 'work–life balance'; and the enormous growth of globalisation which began to bring with it unease, uncertainty and pressure. The period closed with a recognition that the corporate world was prone to disastrous mismanagement – after all, 2006 was the year of the Enron trial, the biggest corporate scandal of the new century – but it also saw the world opening up as never before. That same year Facebook and Twitter ushered in a world in which private lives and professional selves became inextricably linked by a rising tide of social media. The origins of the existential angst many professionals now experience about work can be traced very clearly back to the Mezzanine Years.

Phase three runs from 2007 to 2019, the *Co-Working Years*, in which the great acceleration continued. No one had time to stop to think what it might all mean. The smartphone and laptop heralded the beginning of the end of the office as we know it and co-working became mainstream (the co-working company WeWork started in 2010). Professional workers began to be classified and chased as 'talent'. This era was defined by vaulting technological ambition and scope. The emergent tech companies from Bloomberg to Google raised the bar, making offices citadels of status. Travel budgets and conferences mushroomed; networking online and in person proliferated. Yet these were also the years in which the downsides of the digital world surfaced with Sherry Turkle's hugely influential *Alone Together* published in 2011 putting the atomisation of those who would rather 'text than talk' into the discussion about the social impact of this technology. By 2016 we were in what the World Economic Forum called the famous 'Fourth Industrial Revolution', which predicted, correctly, a massive realignment in the relationships between humans and machines. This was the era when the concept of mindfulness and the desire to switch off became mainstream; reskilling became a major preoccupation and the idea of well-being at work acknowledged the epidemic of work-related stress. But no one anticipated the black swan event of a global pandemic, let alone prepared for it. Far from it. This made 2019 the last year of modern working life as it had been known since 1945.

And so we come to today, to the fourth phase of work, the *Nowhere Office Years*, which is the subject of this book. Beginning in 2020, it represents the working era in which several shifts are happening at once. They may be triggered by the pandemic but their roots precede it.

These shifts are unprecedented precisely because they are happening simultaneously in three key areas: in politics, specifically the issues of inequality and sustainability; in culture, in particular the shift to a working world dominated by Generation Z but in which all generations are still co-workers; and in technology, where between the start of the pandemic and the end of it we have moved from the internet era to what is being called 'the metaverse' (where virtual reality becomes far more real in our lives than we ever thought possible).[12] The Nowhere

Office is a distillation of all of this. It contains crossover from the Optimism Years, the Mezzanine Years and the Co-Working Years but will make its own mark on every aspect of the office – i.e. working life – for years to come.

Six Shifts

I have divided the book into six chapters, each of which addresses a key shift that makes this new Nowhere Office era of work different. Technology does not get a chapter of its own because while the office may be nowhere, technology is everywhere. When tech became the hero of the hour that kept the professional working show on the road, the collective distrust of robots, AI and automation faded. American companies spent $15 billion a week during the pandemic to invest and install technologies connecting home and office while, according to McKinsey, 90 per cent of global services hubs made the transition to a remote delivery model.[13] Each chapter features some historical context to better understand the present and I make some predictions. While the landscape is evolving constantly, some trends for the foreseeable future are already clear. At the back of the book, the chapter called Reinventions offers some practical takeaways.

In 'Shift 1: Placeless, Timeless' the issues of where and when we work are explored within the context of hybrid working becoming the norm in what is arguably the biggest mass workplace experiment ever undertaken. The inconsistencies of current approaches to RTO (return to office) are set against the complexity inherent in matching this with WFH (work from home). The story of the office building, our relationship to it and the pros and cons of it remaining a central fixture of organisational life are all discussed, as is the knock-on effect to cities and central business districts of the shift to different locations for work. Finally, this chapter looks at time, which if we are not careful will continue to get more and not less crunched.[14] It ends by asking whether changing the way we manage and measure time can unlock a new way of working which is much more aligned to the reality of how people want to work now.

'Shift 2: Worker Beings' looks beyond the identity crisis engulfing the office to the identity of the professionals who work in it. Their world is changing as much as the bricks and mortar buildings they work in. It suggests that the old, increasingly fragmented working identities which dominated pre-pandemic work will now be joined by new demographics – the hybrid 'haves and have-nots' and a generational cohort I'm calling Learner, Leaver and Leader. I look at how these different task-based identities exist within the biggest single multi-generational cohort working alongside each other at any time in modern working history. None of these identity shifts happened overnight. But the pandemic catapulted them into view. I predict that identity politics will shift as a result of the new fundamental identities around hybrid work.

'Shift 3: The Productivity Puzzle' frames productivity, that notoriously problematic but vital metric, alongside the new kid on the corporate block, Purpose-with-a-capital-P. It is not surprising at a time of dramatic change that more people are asking why they work and what it means. Who wants all the hassle and stress when they don't even feel they are contributing or producing something useful? This chapter looks at the increasing backlash against work, the rise of the 'Lying Flat' movement, and yet argues that work can and should be not only a source of raw income but also a purposeful life itself, if leaders take heed of the alarm bells ringing loud and clear.

'Shift 4: New Networks' covers one of the biggest shifts in the way we work: how networks will dominate the Nowhere Office and how they have fundamentally moved power from top-down to bottom-up. Shift 4 explores the post-pandemic role of networking conferences and 'in-person' connections and predicts that hybrid models of scaled down IRL (in real life) combined with online interactions will continue. It also assesses the 'diversity dividend' in the context of social capital. This section also asks whether some tricks are being missed in embracing the power of networks and who could win if they changed tack. Finally, this chapter looks at the oldest example of successful professional networking: the long lunch.

'Shift 5: Marzipan Management' addresses arguably the toughest nut to crack in improving professional working life: management. This isn't a chapter about management (or its alter ego leadership) per se, so much as a recognition of the stuck state of working life before the pandemic. It argues that the way we manage not only others but also ourselves has to shift substantially now and that failure to do so will be calamitous. Focusing on two key areas to address – trust and systems – it also makes the case that modern office life has embraced complexity when the exact opposite – simplicity – is required. It looks at the key corporate interface between those who work and those who manage and presents a win-win model for returning the human to 'Human Resources'.

And finally in 'Shift 6: Social Health and Well-being' I want to put the case for a shift towards workplaces which embed the idea of *what functions well* across their organisations. It is time to become far bolder about what we mean by 'wellness' and embrace what I call 'social health'. The definition of health as the presence of wellness, not the absence of injury or disease, is what drives this final shift to move workers towards being 'their best self' in the office, wherever that office is and whenever they work in it.

To help me illustrate all of these dramatic shifts, I turned to Studs Terkel for inspiration. In 1974 (right at the end of the Optimism Years), Terkel interviewed hundreds of disparate workers across the United States and simply recorded their voices, catching the cadence and the hum and the grit of their lived experience. It is Studs Terkel who got me interested in the world of work and people's working lives, and for this reason I decided that the themes in this book might best come alive with a selection of voices from the office world. For this book I conducted over fifty conversations with a wide variety of people across the demographics of Learner, Leaver and Leader: executives, public figures, freelancers, leaders, mainly in the UK and United States but also across the rest of the world. I talked to people working in the creative industries, those working in hospital offices, in back-end operations supporting front-line systems, in one-person start-ups in the Generation Z demographic and Generation X 'solopreneurs'. They helped me build a picture of what working life means to them now and how it could be shaped in the near future.

We never see the future as clearly as we see the past.

It is as if the more seismic the shift the less we anticipate it until it has arrived. For instance, blockchain technology is upending finance as we know it and decentralising centuries of controlled banking – but people said it would never happen. I was one of the naysayers against the driverless car but no one would bet against it now, nor electric vehicles replacing petrol-driven ones. The Nowhere Office is not a blip or a trend which is going to be reversed. I have written this book to help those of us in the professions who are in the middle of the biggest upheaval of our working lives, whether we are Learners, Leavers or Leaders, to help shape the future rather than wait passively for it to happen to us. The issues raised here affect the school office, the factory back office, the farm office and the hospital office just as much as they do the corridors of power in government. They affect the creative communities in advertising and marketing as much as the processing centre of a manufacturing business. For the office is everywhere, despite now being in the middle of nowhere.

I

Shift 1: Placeless, Timeless

Acres of gray steel desk, gray steel filing cabinets, and steel-gray faces under indirect light. One wall is lined with glass-enclosed cubicles for the supervisory personnel. It is all very neat, antiseptic, impersonal. The only human touch is supplied by a bank of IBM machines, clacking away cheerfully in the background.

> Opening scene of *The Apartment*,
> Billy Wilder and I. A. L. Diamond, 1960

An hour, once it lodges in the queer element of the human spirit, may be stretched to fifty or a hundred times its clock length; on the other hand, an hour may be accurately represented on the timepiece of the mind by one second.

> Virginia Woolf, *Orlando*

After the financial crash of 2008, the legendary architect Frank Duffy took a walk around New York and made a prescient observation of how the office, the main symbol of modern working life, might be about to end: 'The building isn't a useful unit of analysis anymore, because organisations are always bigger or smaller and constantly changing. At least half operate in a virtual world, in a placeless world.'[1] Today, in the aftermath of the twenty-first century's first pandemic, we work from the middle of somewhere and nowhere: we work hybrid, we WFH (work from home) or we WFA (work from anywhere).

This chapter looks at the disruption of old norms around two previously immutable aspects of work: fixed time and place. It is only in the last four hundred years at most that the building as the rigidly fixed place for work we now call the office has become a defining feature of professional, administrative work. It does not have to remain so. Hybrid working is in operation to some degree in all but a handful of professional workplaces (with the reminder that while there are many jobs which must be done from a fixed location, such as frontline medical workers or cleaners, they are not the focus of this book). I will look at what the office needs to be, how the home or the mobile working pattern will operate in practice, and frame it all against time, and what Virginia Woolf called 'the timepiece of the mind'.

Office workers are no longer constrained by the physical diktats of place and time. The capability to work from anywhere has existed for a while but the pandemic put rocket boosters on cultural change. Discussions about RTO (returning to the office) are increasingly fraught and in flux. There is no uniform model or agreement. The case for going into an office regularly is having to be made to the workforce and many are rejecting it – risking a huge rise in underused corporate space.[2]

In addition, up to half of America's jobs are projected to be freelance by 2030 and two-thirds of employers now regard some form of remote work or hybrid work as 'the new norm'.[3] Many companies are declaring themselves 'fully remote', meaning they have a competitive edge over those requiring presenteeism. Offices will need to appeal to people differently now they can use a computer anywhere, and nearly everyone has experienced working from home during the lockdowns.

Suddenly the smartphone, which increased from 122 million circulating globally in 2007 to 1,536 million in 2021, has become 'the desk', affecting hundreds of millions of people in terms of their routine, commute, workflow and interactions with colleagues.[4] It also affects hundreds of millions more with the knock-on economic effects on commercial property, infrastructure, hospitality and retail in cities and suburbs.

In this new world time matters as much as place. Cloud-based technology and automation have already kicked open the windows and knocked down the walls of the traditional office, but the digital world swallows up time just as much as the old world did. Microsoft's Trends Survey shows that as much as 42 per cent additional digital exchanges took place when people were working from home during the pandemic.[5]

What is different is that we can now choose how to manage the time we spend working in a way that suits us rather than the traditional nine to five, Monday to Friday routine. This explains why discussions around the four-day week have reached an intensity never seen before. We are not yet anywhere near to the famous fifteen-hour working week John Maynard Keynes predicted in the 1930s, but his prediction seems newly relevant. We do still want to work (and we need to financially) but in new ways.[6]

Emerging from the long tail of Covid something vital and exciting becomes clear: the old normal doesn't exist any more. It is important to recognise that we have entered a liminal in-between time in the history of work.

There have always been changes in work. We can track today's move towards full-blown flexibility back to the six-hour day introduced by industrialist Kellogg in the 1930s. In shortening the working week to enlarge the base of working people, Kellogg's reforms unintentionally triggered the nascent movement for modern work–life balance. The widespread entry of women into office life from the 1960s also prepared the foundations for the modern campaign for greater flexibility which emerged in the 1980s. The 'Fourth Industrial Revolution' of the internet, AI and automation has brought us to the cusp of yet more change, but the pandemic turned incremental change into a surge. Dave Eisenberg of the proptech company Zigg Capital in New York said:

> Covid forced the world into an experiment on remote work as a viable replacement for in-office work for a lot of groups that would never have thought to test the hypothesis. And what they discovered is that while it might not be optimal, it was certainly plausible that if you're in an intellectual pursuit you can actually do your job remotely. For anyone not in a physical service delivery function, and that's a huge chunk of the economy, the remainder of people are able to work remotely in some capacity.

The Fourth Work Shift

As outlined in the introduction, the Nowhere Office can be understood as the fourth phase of work since the end of the Second World War. The first phase is the Optimism Years, 1945–77, the heyday of fixed office life. Then came the Mezzanine Years, 1978–2006, during which issues around flexibility and work–life balance began to build but were never properly addressed. This was also a time that encompassed the furious growth of globalisation in the 1980s and 1990s and ushered in the 'always on' era of working life. During the third phase, the Co-Working Years, 2006–19, mobility arrived for a new demographic armed with ambition and apparently limitless options, Generation Mobile. This new workforce was dubbed #GenMobile. By 2016 data showed that 38 per cent of workers globally prized flexible working,[7] but the prevailing management models remained surprisingly inflexible. Presenteeism was paramount and the reward for working hard was promotion so you could work harder, for more pay and perks, and climb the corporate ladder. What was not prized was the idea of working smarter or even working less. During this period there was little original thinking to imagine office life as anything other than glamorous co-working spaces or smart HQs, bookended by global travel for those in the upper echelons of office life and by trips to the coffee stalls and bars in the vicinity of the city-based office for the rest.

In the fourth phase, the Nowhere Office, beginning in 2020, everything is moving off its old moorings and significant change seems possible. Covid-19 grounded everyone, from the executive constantly shuttling between airports to the desk-bound PA. While working full time from home during pandemic lockdowns was temporary, it has left a sticky residue. It no longer seems right or sensible to work full time from the office. People recognise that their work, and therefore their time, is a valuable commodity and they want to have a greater say in when and where they sell it.

Hardliners and Softliners

It is clear, however, that our attitudes to how we work are complex and inconsistent.[8] Take for instance the Ipsos data that Generation Z and older millennials wish both to work from home three days a week (62 per cent of Generation Z and 56 per cent of millennials) while at the same time wanting (58 per cent of Generation Z and 48 per cent of millennials) to work face to face with colleagues, i.e. from an office.[9]

Forty-two per cent of people with children felt that working from home placed their mental well-being under additional stress, yet 62 per cent say that WFH (working from home) afforded them a better work–life balance.[10]

A huge Vodafone survey showed that 75 per cent of global companies had already introduced some form of hybrid or flexible working post-pandemic before a full return to work.[11] Yet considerable ambivalence remains among some leaders. In one camp you get the hardliners who believe working from the office is best. Many feel that those who work from home are to some extent work-shy. At the very least they wish to penalise people who prefer to work hybrid. Take the bombastic internal memo sent by James Gorman, chairman and CEO of Morgan Stanley to his staff: 'If you want to get paid New York rates, you work in New York. None of this "I'm in Colorado . . . and getting paid like I'm sitting in New York City"',[12] echoing an equally robust statement from David Solomon of Goldman Sachs that working from home was 'an aberration'.[13] Similarly the veteran Wall Street observer William Cohan simply said this: 'Here's my advice to you, fellow Wall Street drones: Get back to the office.'[14] In another camp are the more emollient hybrid softliners such as Kevin Ellis, London-based chairman of consultancy firm PwC with 285,000 employees in 155 countries around the world, who said that 'we want to enshrine new working patterns so that they outlast the pandemic'.[15] Regardless of which camp employers are in, it is obviously true that an awful lot of social capital resides in the office. I talked to Kevin Ellis, who said: 'My worry is that we're going to create a glass ceiling for people whose careers will be stunted because they're working from home and not realising what they're missing out on.'

Nevertheless, all of these comments reflect a wistfulness on the part of big business which can no longer magically attract the same kind of worker prepared to work in the same way they did before the pandemic.[16] Hybrid working reflects the fact that mobility and freedom are the new prizes for the professional working class, who do not so much want to 'clock on' and 'clock off' as move seamlessly between work and private life. The shift to a placeless and timeless dimension for work means the fixed HQ will have to work a lot harder to attract and retain 'talent'. As Tim Chapman, founder and CEO of Leesman who measure employee workplace experience, wrote towards the end of 2021, 'Covid-19 has upended business's historic operational and financial justifications for workplace.'[17]

Castles in the Air

We have shifted very far from the moment in 2017, ahead of the opening of the 3.2-acre site of its new European head-quarters on the old Roman ruins at Watling Street in the heart of the City of London, when Michael Bloomberg declared:

> This building is designed for our employees. So that they can be productive and happy in their environment and be proud of where they work. And then for visitors – for customers, for prospective employees, friends and relatives. You want people to walk out and say 'I want to work there' or 'I want to deal with this company.'

The architects Foster + Partners say that they designed it so that 'Everyone passes through this animated space, increasing the likelihood of chance meetings and informal discussions.'

The message was that 'placeless' might be a concept and technologically possible – but place matters. An ostentatiously powerful place was good for business and attracting people to work for you. But the pandemic changed perceptions. Lingering Covid-related health and safety fears around building ventilation may make chance meetings less attractive than they were before. Every big building has elevators which have echoes of the commuter crush and cause uncertainty over the dangers of physical proximity. Being in an office may even trigger feelings we don't want – of being unsure and unsafe. Le Corbusier's quest for 'inner cleanness' came directly out of the new public health aesthetics following the Spanish Flu outbreak of 1918–20. Would Foster + Partners be given the same commission by Bloomberg in 2023 or 2033? Just as the Spanish Flu influenced architectural design for clean, safe minimalism, the pandemic has sparked a different aesthetic entirely. Now properties are being repurposed to reduce shared dining tables and kitchens, gyms and showers, and clever spaces to meet semi-socially and semi-collaboratively are being rethought to enable social distancing. Will Bloomberg build another gigantic palace like Watling Street? Probably not.

Bloomberg's story is instructive because for so long it defined city-based corporate offices as palaces of opulence and comfort which encouraged presenteeism. It pioneered the all-you-can-eat buffets, the glittering digital displays and hi-tech hi-touch beanbag era of the Co-Working Years. Office life was glamorous, it had status, it was opulent, and it was fun. Until it wasn't.

Now the fun is tempered not only with a sense that office life is restrictive and confining, but that it brings with it complication and risk. Thus the appeal of remote-based work grows. Companies like Firstbase, which promotes remote-based teams, bring a breathless enthusiasm to the idea that no one should have a place to work from: 'Being handcuffed to an office and expected to live in a high cost of living city with a low quality of life is a remnant of the industrial revolution,' declares its website.

The old kind of office was a place where you were metaphorically handcuffed, primarily by technology, even when this was simply a typewriter or a filing cabinet. Property giant Cushman & Wakefield entered into a significant strategic partnership with WeWork in the summer of 2021 as if to underscore that the old divisions between long-term office use and more flexible use are now intertwined.[18]

Smart leaders today are thinking the unthinkable and asking whether they need an office in the same way again, not because they are following the hybrid herd, but because they are keeping their eyes and ears open to what is going on in their own businesses. Joanna Swash, CEO of outsourcing reception, PA and communications provider Moneypenny (and a member of the Forbes Business Council), was frank that her perceptions had been challenged by the pandemic when everyone had to go fully remote overnight:

> Before Covid-19 I thought we've got amazing offices, and that they are this space that everybody loves. What I learned was that our culture was so strong that it wasn't just based on the office or on the physical environment, but it was based on that whole community feel, and how people trust each other. It should have been obvious to me, but that was a really big lesson at the start of the pandemic.

A similar point was made by Chris Thurling, chair of Armadillo, a digital design firm which went fully remote during the pandemic, and who expanded his business during this period:

> I want to remain completely open-minded about whether we ever need to have a traditional office again. If you look at the performance of our business since March 2020, we

are performing really well and our clients are not saying there's been a drop-off in quality. Our profitability as a business has gone up and we're growing. Why would we change too much?

Presenteeism, Incorrect

The desire to attract workers back to offices explains the growth in what has been called 'the smart-building trend', where companies are vying to attract and retain office-based workers with running tracks on the roof or all-year outdoor terraces in addition to back-to-work bonuses and of course those all-you-can-eat buffets and en-suite gyms.[19] It is certainly one way to keep architects, designers and landlords productive but it masks the real purpose behind it: presenteeism.

Of course not every job can be remote as industries and sectors vary hugely. You cannot compare a workplace which is reliant only on telephone and computer to one that requires more than that. In some areas of working life dealing with complex real-time issues needs to be done face to face. But for most of corporate life the pandemic has proved that it is very possible to keep teams and projects working using teleconferencing and the internet. The Nowhere Office can and should enable the way we prioritise location and shift from presenteeism as a rule to presenteeism as an exception. Or to use immersion instead – sudden blitzes of brainstorms and meetings rather like an in-house conference. This is already the model many businesses have pivoted to.

Bruce Daisley, an authority on the future of work and presenter of the podcast 'Eat Sleep Work Repeat' watches the trend closely. He told me:

Probably the most farsighted approach I have seen was Dropbox which said late in 2020 that getting people into the office for a certain number of days or specific days doesn't work. Because people think, why am I going in to the office on Wednesday? Just because it's Wednesday doesn't make any sense. People will come in to the office when they need to and they will come in to the office for experiences.[20]

People will not come into the office, however, under duress. And if they do come, they will not stay loyal for long. In the summer of 2021 Google faced significant employee discontent when it announced that it intended to use its pay calculator to implement pay according to proximity to the office, reflecting the priority some employers still put on presentee-ism.[21] This strategy is risky and unfair as Sarah O'Connor commented in the *Financial Times*:

> If two workers from the same head office want to switch to working from home, but one inherited a house in an expensive city while the other had been living in a commuter town, is it fair for the latter to take a pay cut?[22]

She quoted Mark Zuckerberg of Meta telling his employees by video: 'We'll adjust salary to location . . . There'll be severe ramifications for people who are not honest about this.' But who is not being honest? Some companies are clearly struggling to accept the serious shift in mindset and values of their talent. It remains to be seen whether management will rise to the challenges of supporting home-based working or continue to believe they can persuade and cajole workers to be present in the office when they don't want to be. There was a pushback experienced by other major companies such as Apple, which found itself forced to row back from dictating office working days post-pandemic.[23]

Anne-Elisabeth Moutet, a French broadcaster and columnist based in Paris, understands presenteeism as something else too: a feature of power politics:

> The French system hates hybrid. Because the French boss wants to know what his subordinates are doing, very micro-managing most of the time. A strict hierarchy prevails. And the fact that this hierarchy actually doesn't really work with the new ways of [hybrid] working means that innovation is slower in our country; sometimes it's even sabotaged by people next to you who are vying with you for the boss's attention. If this sounds like the court of a minor Borgia or Louis XIV, minus the decor, that's where it comes from.

It was the eighteenth-century French economist Jacques Claude Marie Vincent de Gournay who coined the term *bureaucracy* on which office life is founded. The office now has to learn to ditch its petty bureaucracy in order to reform and refit for purpose. Being placeless and timeless has to become embedded in the coding of the workplace, replacing presenteeism and working round the clock. A good office is always about more than place. Both Moneypenny and Armadillo embody businesses which cherish their workers because they acknowledge how much they need them and work to serve both them and their clients. They keep open-minded and adapt continuously. They don't build grand palaces of presenteeism and they are prepared to do without them if that is what their workers want.

In the end the question for leaders who want their people back in the office is: why? Is it because regulating some work from home – finance especially – is legally complex? Is it optics? That management and leaders feel emotionally invested in high-spec, high-tech, visible offices? Or is it a failure to comprehend the scale and sweep of change? However, luckily for property developers and those who like offices or can't replace them easily, we have not reached the end of the office for a couple of important reasons.

Built-in Birdsong

First, the office will not disappear, because people need to be around each other physically for all sorts of reasons and in all kinds of ways. And here is Kevin Ellis again: 'When I'm in the office I can probably speak to five people in an hour. Just wandering around their desks. There is a kind of birdsong of the office. Everyone's saying, good morning. How you doing today?'

Birdsong is a powerful way to describe the unique communication between humans – the exchange of knowledge, opinion, information, intelligence and emotion, and this is impossible to fully capture or replicate digitally.

Mohit Bakaya, controller of BBC Radio 4, emphasised the value of office IRL (in real life) to me like this: 'Creative conversations happen in the corridor. It's someone perching on the desk saying "oh, you have to read this or that".' He described the creative collaboration that happens serendipitously in the office, which cannot be measured precisely. And everyone knows that osmotic exchanges of skills and connection happen unprompted, unplanned and in person.

Clearly not everything can be offset by collaborative technology, which is another argument for some form of routine presence back in the office. That said, cloud-based collaboration software before Covid-19 had become like social media:

often more time-wasting than time-saving, blocked by chat and chatter, with a rather ungoverned set of different, often competing platforms that made some aspects of workflow management great and others clogged and confusing. What was required for actual output and productivity and what was chat often had no clear distinction. In *Cubed: A Secret History of the Workplace* Nikil Saval memorably describes 'excessive sociability and inane attentiveness to others'. The total employee communications software market is set to exceed $1,780 million by 2027, but a large proportion of this market is still not fun or productive to use. The next phase is likely to be more focused on enabling better real-time but remote collaboration.[24] Josh Greene, who used to be in the senior leadership team at WeWork before creating Groove,[25] his own start-up, makes the point about how technology away from an office needs to mimic the old norms of when people sat side by side:

> People don't feel part of anything in their work or not enough, and hybrid working increases this alienation. We're focusing on building a more informal, more evolved kind of interface for people to connect with each other as during real-time online use. I like to say it's like Slack for the TikTok generation. People's expectations are now mobile, their expectations are immersive, their expectations are customisable, which factors in feedback, ideas, a jam over twenty minutes of coffee or its digital equivalent. People want profound, small, short interactions and new social platforms which mimic those interactions and networks as consciously designed as possible.

Where teams are genuinely remote this kind of innovation is welcome. Yet large organisations need their people to be in for more reasons than desk-based collaboration. Ben Page, Global CEO of market research firm Ipsos, which employs 18,000 people, explains:

> We still need offices – we just don't need them for work. Most businesses have now discovered that we need them for serendipity, for team meetings and collaboration, but not to sit there checking things. But we do need them for training, for building a culture. I now employ hundreds of [people], who've never physically been to any of our offices, and that worries me because they don't really know what the zeitgeist of the business is.

His view echoes McKinsey's data from nine countries and 800 CEOs, which shows clearly that not all jobs can be done remotely, nor can all be done best online, among them coaching, teaching, mentoring.[26] Offices will therefore become critical places for learning, training and development in a far more original and constant way than before. This is something that can and should be done in person, with others, to aid collaboration and foster community spirit. Additionally, simple loneliness is something that offices can mitigate: isolation is obviously not good for people, and if your employer or your client provides a social setting so much the better. The Scottish broadcaster and writer Ayesha Hazarika who shuttled for years pre-pandemic in her 'mobile office – an Uber' – struggled when she was locked at home by the pandemic and felt 'rescued from talking to my plants and my toaster when I got a broadcasting gig at Times Radio in early 2021 which meant I got to go into a studio some of the time. Even having a fixed place to go to a couple of days a week was something of a lifesaver.'

Better Coffee

The second strength of the office is comfort. Not everyone wants to work from home, and not everyone can do so easily. The inequalities of class and income don't disappear in the Nowhere Office, if anything they become more visible. Not everyone has space for a home office or noise-free environments or even sufficient internet connection speeds. A study by the Quality of Life Foundation in the UK concluded that key among place-based quality of life is 'connectivity, mix of uses, aesthetics, maintenance and safety'.[27] For those without well-equipped or comfortable homes, the office provides everything from great coffee and a place to shower to super-fast broadband. Dave Eisenberg, the property analyst, says that the benefits of not commuting and remote working may be outweighed by the unique asset of a non-home environment from which to work:

> In relative terms of the cost of people, especially highly paid, talented people, the cost of real estate is so small that I would rather actually spend more money on the office environment to make it more of an amenity, where we have great food that's provided or we have great exercise facilities, or even great air and we have certainly the collegial components of getting people together. We're just going to make the office better than it was.

Elsbeth Johnson, one of the key thinkers on organisational behaviour at MIT and the author of *Step Up, Step Back*, told me:

> During the pandemic a lot of my knowledge-worker clients wanted to go back to the office and be together. Why?

Simple: they missed being with each other and doing the work that really can only be done face to face. There were a number of drivers behind this. First and foremost, these people really like the work they do and the firm they work for. These offices aren't the kind of 'David Brent' set-ups where bosses are monitoring people while they do boring, meaningless work. Second, these people really like each other – their colleagues are often friends. This work 'family' is important to them and they've missed it. And, thirdly – and very importantly – their offices are very pleasant places to be. They're well-designed spaces, in which the firm has invested money and care. So whether it's because of the layout, or the quality of the coffee machine, or the fact there's an onsite doctor or gym, there is real value for people in being in the office rather than working from home. That's even truer for younger members of staff, many of whom will have been living and working out of their bedrooms in house-shares, and for whom the office is therefore an even more attractive alternative.

Notwithstanding the case for why we still need offices in a repurposed way, the Nowhere Office brings huge uncertainty to those paying for costly real estate. There is probably simply too much of it relative to those who will inhabit it on an affordable basis. The ratios are now all wrong.[28] Those invested in corporate office space have to work a lot harder to keep people there. A year after Bloomberg's London HQ opened Goldman Sachs entered into a twenty-five-year lease for a £1-billion building a mile away on Plumtree Court: it comprises well over 750,000 square feet of office space, which includes the largest trading floor in London and onsite lactation suites for breastfeeding mothers. That is a huge investment in presenteeism. Different sectors require different levels of presenteeism of course (and Goldman Sachs and the financial sector can justly make some claim here due to the nature of the work) but in future the majority of offices are going to shapeshift to fit the new hybrid era. Many will be replaced at least some of the time by office proxies, extending a trend that began before the pandemic – private members clubs, coffee shops and co-working specific spaces such as WeWork. But now the biggest competitor of all will be people's homes.

The Airlock and the Airing Cupboard

J. K. Rowling's fictional ex-army London detective Cormoran Strike limps on his prosthetic leg up to a makeshift bed in his beaten-up Soho detective agency because he doesn't really have any other life than work. His work is his life so his office is his home. One reason why people put up with commuting for so long was precisely because they wanted a demarcation between both places. Only a rather desperate character, it seems, wants to sleep at the office. The pandemic changed that. Home, briefly – but long enough to change habits and perspectives – became the office on a wholesale basis. The focus flipped from going 'to' the office to WFH – working from home.

Post-pandemic the trend is clear. People want the choice and organisations are turning to hybrid working. There is currently no norm or standardisation but the expectation is that a three-day office week of some kind and a two-day WFH may become the norm. It is forty years since novelist William Gibson first coined the phrase 'cyberspace' and now the internet and the fibre-optic cable mean we live and work in it with no barrier in between. As the sociologist Doreen Massey memorably asked in 1991 (the middle of the Mezzanine Years):

'Can't we rethink our sense of place? A sense of place which is adequate to this era of time-space compression?'[29] Well, it turns out, we can.

The impact of the new boundaries can be seen clearly in the way in which the traditional linear career for professionals is being challenged by the Nowhere Office. Herminia Ibarra of London Business School says that: 'Hybrid will drive an even clearer divide between the traditional, ladder careers and the squiggly ones.'[30]

The challenges of a hybrid working life for 'squiggly' careers are not only logistical but also involve huge unanswered questions about a plethora of issues from tax to technology to boundaries. How do you create a personal space when you do your work from where you live? Mohit Bakaya calls it 'the airlock'. The need for mental discipline to put in barriers between work and home. This is especially true when concentration is digitally disrupted so continuously. The famous study by Gloria Mark at the University of California, Irvine, showing that it takes twenty-three minutes and fifteen seconds to regain concentration when coming off the internet, is compelling.[31]

Nicholas Bloom of Stanford University, a scholar whose work has previously championed the benefits of working from home, noted in a new study as the pandemic got underway that children, space, privacy and choice were all undermining previous productivity gains associated with the 'telecommuting' work movement (what WFH used to be called).[32] Nevertheless, despite reservations, Bloom and colleagues surveyed 22,500 Americans in 2020 to assess how much working from home would 'stick' post Covid-19, and concluded that on balance the benefits did outweigh the drawbacks.

It could be argued that the digital era has already broken down the barrier between home and work life because social networks, shopping, email, text are all enabled by the same technology, our smartphones. So why not make the best of it? Bejay Mulenga, twenty-six, an award-winning social entre-preneur and digital savant sitting in his home in Shoreditch, London set up a foodbank for 20,000 people who entered poverty due to the jobs crash. He also runs a highly successful digital marketing business and says:

> I've had various different types of offices in the last six to eight years. But since 2019, I'd invested in space in my home as I had a spare room and my living room and lounge. For headspace I found I wanted to be able to work from home on some days. So recent events just accelerated my investment in my home office, which now means I actually can do work from here. I can do paid work, and I've created income streams that didn't exist for myself before, like creating digital products.

The idea of 'headspace' is key here. The London-based Norwegian-Nigerian entrepreneur and investor Tom Adeyoola, who successfully founded and sold *Metail*, a sustainable digital fashion technology start-up operating in the Asia-Pacific region and Europe and with over two hundred employees, subcon-tractors and remote-based workers spanning engineering and manufacturing, design, sales and marketing, told me:

> Engineers like to work in a quiet space, and then they go into other rooms to be noisy, whereas more creative types like to be in a noisy space, and they go into rooms to be quiet. So there's a clash between them, but you want to try and create the ability for them to connect in ways which are low friction. So how can you do that? We spent a lot of time trying to create ways on Skype, or now Zoom rooms, where you could just walk in digitally, which still

gave a sense of connectivity. In other words, experimenting with ways to use digital in a similar way to physical space, with the equivalent of 'do not disturb' for those who need it, while still being reachable and connected to what else is happening if they are needed.

What all of this clearly adds up to is that hybrid working is fiendishly complex and has to be iterative. For all of its faults there was a simplicity about working from one fixed place with regular hours. The sociologist Arlie Russell Hochschild's work, such as her book *The Time Bind*, published in 1997, consistently articulates the frictions involved in trying to combine work and home life. She has written of: 'The emotional magnets beneath home and workplace are in the process of being reversed. Work has become a form of "home" and home has become work.'[33]

Although as I've said earlier Generation Z wants the best of both worlds, they too feel the pinch when it comes to managing boundaries. Yasmina Memarian, twenty-six, a half-Italian, half-Iranian editorial social media manager based in the UK for The LEGO Group, articulated the daily paradoxes of her new normal to me like this:

The downside of working from home has been work–life balance which has become a blur. I also think that short coffee breaks in the office that lend themselves to quick but useful check-ins and questions have now become a clutter of Teams messages and online meetings, so without doubt the days end up becoming longer.

When you don't have a fixed beginning, middle and end to your day, when the boundary wall between 'the office' may be the den or the kitchen counter, you need skills, willpower and privacy – all of which need to be negotiated not just with an employer, but with yourself, your family and your co-workers.

#GenMobile

The home, or the co-working space, the coffee shop, or for the lucky few the tropical island: these are the competitors to presenteeism-based office life. This is partly because mobility is hardwired into us. We like to be on the move. The question of movement, the flow of people from one place to another, has always been fundamental to the story of work itself.

The interruptions and reconfigurations that have happened recently are therefore a vital part of the story. During the Covid-19 crisis the amount of money spent on business travel fell by $700 billion and it produced fairly widespread reassessments among executives who had previously been almost permanently in transit.[34]

Eric Hazan, one of McKinsey's leading experts on the future of work, lives in Paris but handles many global clients and immediately noticed that:

> My identity was one of a travelling executive. I have a French client that owns a subsidiary in the US with headquarters in Chicago. Up until 2020, we had a steering committee meeting with the executive committee every month to ensure the smooth running of the project we were working on. We made a monthly trip to Chicago to attend these meetings. Looking back, we could have done it remotely, but we didn't because that was not common practice at the time.

Eric Hazan's experience was echoed by Niall Murphy, a Swiss-based South African who before the pandemic was constantly travelling as the CEO of EVRYTHNG, a trans-Atlantic software company. He told me:

> Personally my life is much improved with less travel and more remote work. I've lost a lot of weight. I'm sleeping in the same time zone consistently and am more rested and productive for it. I'm doing regular exercise. I'm able to enjoy my environment a lot more. I expect to be travelling a lot less, but when I do for longer periods it will be so that I can invest time in relationship building. Transactional travel is replaced by Zoom. Previously my life involved weekly flights to offices in London or New York, or to meet customers, partners and investors in the US, Europe and Asia. The expectation of being physically present with colleagues or business partners at high frequency has obviously disappeared, and I doubt it'll return in the same way it existed before.

Commuter transport also took a gigantic hit. One year into the global grip of Covid-19, Transport for London, which runs the city's buses and tube trains, needed a £1.08 billion bailout;[35] in New York the MTA, which runs the subway, was awarded $4 billion in the 2020 Covid stimulus bill. Although inevitably the numbers of passengers began to creep back up and down again following the up and down cycles of the coronavirus, commuting and business travel have become seen as largely expendable by many people.

The biggest beneficiaries of the shift to placelessness are the true digital nomads, those who can up sticks and relocate anywhere there is broadband. Typically this means those without children or other caring responsibilities, i.e. Generation

Z and anyone else who fits that bill. Digital nomads must also be digital natives for whom technology holds only promise, not a need for training. Again this tends to favour certain ages over others. Mobility has always represented freedom. Today's model of working from mountaintops and beaches first became widely popular in 2007, inspired by Tim Ferriss's *The 4-Hour Work Week*. The book, which stayed on the bestseller list for seven years and made a zeitgeist millionaire out of Ferriss, coincided with the year the iPhone was born, Netflix streaming gained wings, and texting became 'a thing'. By the following year GPS use was widespread, Android vastly increased the use of mobiles, cloud-based storage went mainstream with Dropbox, and Airbnb was born. The Co-Working Years made mobility part of our mindset and set in motion the end of the office as we know it.

Ignoring hybrid is not an option, not least because by 2030 the majority of the office-based working community is likely to be freelance in the United States and therefore working flexibly, hybrid and in the Nowhere Office.[36] The data is reflected globally: the UK and Brazil are the second and third largest freelance communities with Pakistan, India, Philippines and Bangladesh all seeing sharp rises; most of these freelancers will be digital nomads.[37]

Sir Martin Sorrell, who founded advertising behemoth WPP and now runs the growing global digital brand Media.Monks, gave me this view of the new working landscape:

> Apart from the destruction, which was terrible for people personally, all the pandemic did was just speed up change. San Francisco had problems because apartments were too pricey, a lot of homeless people. California was increasing taxes. The mobility to Colorado or Texas or Florida was going to happen anyway. If you think about all the trends,

flexible career team, distance working, different floor plates in offices, C-19 caused a massive tsunami around that. Our people are digital natives. They aren't even digital first. I don't know whether it's permanent but we're going to assume that people want to be out of the office.

The trend is clear: people want to be out and about, visiting offices but also working from home, or working from nowhere you could call a traditional office in a base which suits them. All of which impacts dramatically on the places where offices used to be: the city.

Busytown and the End of the Commute

The American author Richard Scarry sold 100 million books, most depicting scenes of working life through funny, poignant, wacky creatures ('Lowly Worm' and 'Sally Cat') who are always busy, and always working. In one of my favourites, *What Do People Do All Day?*, one character, 'Able Baker', is a mouse who is always dwarfed by a series of gigantic ovens and loaves. Another, 'Mr Fixit', is a fox who repairs things like cars which are really pickles or pencils. These creatures work in 'Busytown'. Of course in order to get to Busytown, you had to commute. But we don't want to go to Busytown any more. There is consistent data showing that 80 per cent of workers feel the commute is a powerful reason to WFH and not go into an office.[38] Before Covid-19 arrived ordinary office workers endured an average sixty-minute daily commute.[39]

Although the commute is not a wholly negative experience, and can be a useful buffer between home and work, the truth is that we have all outgrown the time-suck of non-essential travel, and the placeless, timeless world makes a daily commute seem pointless. This is also key to the shift to the Nowhere Office: the inconvenience, the sheer folly of certain ways of working, makes the case powerfully: it does not have to be like this. The shift away from place-based purchasing to digital is an illustration of how convenience and speed is replacing old models. Online purchases rose 6–10 per cent globally during the pandemic across most categories according to data compiled by UNCTAD, the United Nations Conference on Trade and Development.[40] This substantially alters the layout of retail spaces and the shift in many cases from office space to warehouse space.

Entrepreneurs who can shift their working patterns away from a city-centre office to a convenience-based model, which does the job regardless of location, are evident wherever you look. Dan Newman, an American who lives in Italy and runs Matter Group, a leading facilitation consultancy, has designed a Nowhere Office to suit not just his needs but those of his co-workers:

> My workplace is in Rome. It serves as an office for my seven colleagues and me. We reopened three days a week where we work together. We continue to work two days remotely. Several of us commute (one colleague from Turin, another from Mantova, myself from Tuscany). It certainly suits our lifestyle.

Australian Jo Scard, who runs a fully remote communications business in Canberra, says that the lack of transport infrastructure and scale of Australia has meant that the post-commute trend was well prepared for:

> Historically, we were sort of prepared, broadband was adopted early. When I purchased my farm fourteen years

ago, the first thing I did when I got out of the car was check mobile reception. To begin with people would say to me 'Gee, I wish I could work like that, not in a city, avoiding the commute.' Now it's becoming normal, you don't have to disguise hybrid working or remote working or pass it off as something which needs excusing. It's the commute which needs a serious justification now.

The most obvious result of the unwillingness to commute is the renewed popularity of the suburbs. The flight to suburbia has accounted for a rise in the property market for residences outside city centres such that rent is projected to decrease 1.2 per cent in Los Angeles' Koreatown and increase 9.9 per cent in the Rancho Cucamonga and San Bernardino district of the Inland Empire.[41] As Dave Eisenberg, of proptech company Zigg Capital, put it, we know that 'high painful commute' locations will suffer in terms of real estate. If you don't have to commute, why should you?

The Nowhere Office can't lead a retreat from the city, without us acknowledging that there are real, long-term costs in doing so. It is cities, after all, in which creativity, the arts, diverse social scenes flourish best. Still, in the short term, the power of the 'central business district' (CBD), the city-based nexus of businesses located around transport hubs and shops and suppliers stretching from the Chicago Loop to Chang Mai Business Park, is waning. Their loss is – for now – suburbia's gain. There was also a noticeable uptick in local newspaper groups' recruitment of journalists in the UK in 2021 as more people worked locally and began to take a greater interest in what was happening on their doorstep.[42]

For cities to attract and retain people, as places both to live and work, they will need to redesign the CBD completely. It will have to become much more mixed-use, residential, artisanal and flexible in its use of space. We may see less of the kind of services that people can get locally, like the shoe-repair shop and locksmith, and instead have more of what people may need in their mini-commutes such as drop-in medical centres, career advice shops and more fitness centres and hybrid live/work spaces.

The CBD may in fact become as outdated as out-of-town malls have become. Their time was up thanks to the internet. Now the CBD in a city may have to compete with the local high street,[43] which has long languished but is now benefiting from two things: first, a rise in footfall from hybrid workers and second, the arrival of hyperlocal pop-up co-working hubs. Two such examples are Soho Studios from Soho House in the UK,[44] and in the US the interesting collaboration between Saks and WeWork (dubbed 'Sakswork').[45]

For individual workers the cost of travel is likely to remain dominant in determining trends of where people work and when. Cost-savings during lockdowns are being replaced by cost-increases on returning to the office. Substantial rises in energy prices and taxes on polluting petrol and diesel vehicles are deterrents.[46] In addition, the pricing models of commuter transport will need to be radically revisited and no doubt subsidised as hybrid continues. Overall we will see a more self-aware, self-conscious professional class emerging for whom every journey is counted and costed not only in raw economic terms but also in terms of effort and reward. And the biggest reward for many is time itself.

Time's Arrow

Time threads constantly through the question of how we work and how we live. The way we value time has increasingly become a driver of why we do what we do. Does it take up too much time? Does it waste time? Is it time, to coin a phrase, *well spent*? Then there is measurement. One study put the commuting time saved at twenty-four days a year.[47] The global productivity management software market is over $40 billion a year and set to grow by 14 per cent by 2028.[48] A large part of this reflects an obsession with time and time management. The modern measurement of time links directly to industrialisation and to the standardisation of time around railway schedules in the late nineteenth century. Shoot forwards to the financial crash of 2008 and huge investments were made in developing technology that kept traders a fraction of a second ahead of others. Time has always counted commercially.

Increasingly it is the personal value of time that matters. For many workers, especially those juggling caring responsibilities, time is constantly short. But executives, forced to stop rushing around during lockdowns, also began to think very differently about how we spend time. They began to not want to be quite so busy. The philosopher Bertrand Russell remarked in 'In Praise of Idleness' in 1932 that 'It will be said that, while a little leisure is pleasant, men would not know how to fill their days if they only had four hours of work out of twenty-four.'[49] Well, Generation Mobile is far keener on leisure than its predecessors. Although working hours have declined globally in the last hundred years, the modern harassed office worker doesn't feel like they have much leisure.[50] Burnout is back for the first time since the 1970s.

When people attended meetings on Zoom during the pandemic they did not take up less time. Data from the University of Chicago's Becker Friedman Institute in May 2021 showed there was a 30 per cent increase in hours worked, 18 per cent of them beyond normal working hours.[51] For this reason the question of an officially shortened working week has gained traction. Scotland, Spain, Iceland and even Japan with its long hours culture have started to create policies promoting the idea of a four-day week on the grounds that less work will reduce the endemic stress that besets the working world and be fairer on women with children who have always been disproportionately penalised by a full-time presenteeism culture.[52]

Naturally the issue around a four-day week or any other standardised model of time is whether the jobs actually fit the schedule. Many mothers returning to work part time are familiar with the scenario of squeezing a full-time job into part-time hours. And it is worth emphasising that not every office worker is in a job that allows them to be away from a desk much at all.

The hybrid world advanced by Covid-19 has done more for flexible and part-time working than decades of campaigning. By autumn 2021 the UK government was consulting on an amendment to its 'right to request' flexible working from starting after six months' employment to beginning immediately.[53] Research by the Boston College Center for Work and Family shows that 87 per cent of employees feel that flexible working improves productivity.[54] However, markedly fewer managers – 70 per cent – think so. That gap signifies the need to identify what does and does not work rather than impose new norms that fail as badly as the old ones. There also needs to be transparency and honesty between employers and employees. Do you want to work part time or do you want to work flexibly? They are not the same thing.

There are three other issues about time and work to consider in the Nowhere Office. The first is that time spent should matter less than outcomes. Should it actually matter whether it takes you two hours or two weeks to get the job done if you bring value to your work and workplace, which can be measured and valued by colleagues and some form of agreed metrics? This is surely the moment to try this more widely. As Professor Lynda Gratton of London Business School who heads up the World Economic Forum's Global Future Council on the New Agenda for Work, Wages and Job Creation[55] puts it: 'to make hybrid a success, you will have to reimagine projects and workflows'.[56] She and her colleague Andrew Scott have redefined time in terms of the lifeline of work, identifying 'the 100 year life' and it is instructive to recognise there are no norms any more: just new demographics, new models, new possibilities. This should be a relief rather than a threat to managers and employees.

The second issue is around time zones. If you imagine we have a placeless world in which you can work in different time zones, using digital cloud-based tools, augmented reality and teleworking, it may be time to lift the lid off the idea that the professional classes only work during the day. It ought to be possible for people to design working patterns where they can work in offices staffed 24/7 as part of the shift in norms around time and place in much the same way that some food and energy outlets or supply chain logistics operate overnight.

The third issue is that we must become more, not less, scrupulous about time management. It is very easy to let time drift away from us when it is stubbornly finite. Despite a plethora of productivity apps sweeping the market, despite increasing life expectancy, the availability of time by the hour, day or week does not increase beyond 168 hours in total (including time to sleep).

So we have to go back to the idea of schedules and time management and look at what does and doesn't work. This means a model of constant test and learn system until the Nowhere Office has been modelled and understood better. Will a standardisation take root, a global norm of three days in the office and two at home? Will the 'Work Unbound' model of employee-owned engineering and design firm ARUP, which allowed 6,000 UK workers – over half of its 15,000 workforce globally – to take part in an experiment to work their hours flexibly between Monday and Sunday, catch on?[57]

Will the 22,000 UK workers of PwC who can work three days a week from home react differently to the Apple workers who resisted this same move so strongly that the company had to back down? Who knows? It is important to price in time for failure – to notice what does not work as well as what does. The datasets on what works with hybrid time management need time to accrue. And what about the 80,000 workers of Fujitsu in Japan who are now, thanks to a programme called Work Life Shift, largely remote-based?[58] Will they dislodge centuries of a working culture which used to be so onerous that pre-pandemic workers took just over half the annual leave they were entitled to?[59] In 2015 a survey by the Japan Institute for Labour Policy and Training showed that over a third of women and men were anxious about 'the ambiguity of work and time off' which teleworking and remote working represented.

Anxiety is increasing and not decreasing. Too much choice, too much transition into the Nowhere Office may feel too much for some people, and much more complicated than the old norm of fixed-place-fixed-hours for others, even if the concept of hybrid is appealing. The risk is that in embracing the limitless options of the liminal moment we are in, we create an identity crisis, not just for work, but for ourselves.

2

Shift 2: Worker Beings

Since we are many selves, changing is not a process of swapping one identity for another but rather a transition process in which we reconfigure the full set of possibilities.

Herminia Ibarra, *Working Identity*

It's going to be pretty messy. It's going to come down to how do we want to work as individuals.

Jonathan Lister, VP of Sales at LinkedIn,
Bloomberg Work Summit, spring 2021

Working life has always had its uniforms and its job titles which say 'This is what we do.' There is a stock photograph on the Alamy photo archive taken in the 1880s of a woman seated in a full-hooped crinoline skirt at a desk in front of a Hammond typewriter, a beautiful machine designed to work as harmoniously and elegantly as a musical instrument. The caption reads 'Typewriter'. Until recently it was not much different – the job titles themselves might have changed and we might have a business card to go with it if we were lucky – but we were still very much defined by what we did.

As the snow globe is shaken, however, and the Nowhere Office emerges with a person rather than a role or a place at its symbolic centre, the identity of professional work is undergoing a profound change. How can work accommodate such vast shifts in patterns of work? What impact does this have on the identity of people who used to have clear job labels, linear schedules and a fixed place of work? The aftershocks of a period during which offices the world over opened, shut and reopened again, like a series of canal lock gates, created a mass shift away from the fixed norms of office life. Inevitably this casts a different light on pre-pandemic preoccupations about identity, in and outside the workplace. While the intense focus on gender, as expressed in people's pronoun preferences, or ethnicity are issues which continue to be important there are other new priorities in the Nowhere Office. New identities will emerge around who has agency to work flexibly, in a way which suits them and allows them to live complete lives – and those who do not. They will be about whether you are an 'émigré' able to choose your new hybrid patterns of work to suit yourself, or a powerless 'economic migrant', forced to take what is given to you on any terms.

This chapter looks at the redrawing of these new identity boundaries and looks ahead to reinventing the identity of work itself.

Lifestyle Incorporated

Fashion has always been a useful prism through which to look at identity at work. As we begin to emerge from a period in which business cards and business suits have lain dormant for over two years, a survey for Cotton Incorporated cotton manufacturers found that 70 per cent of respondents said they would choose a job allowing leisurewear over formal office clothing.[1] The rise of casual 'athleisurewear' by over 80 per cent during the pandemic has led to a series of 'category curveballs' in clothing, as one fashion executive put it.[2] Decades of 'Dress

Down Friday' in which wearing an unbuttoned shirt to work was deemed radical have been replaced by 'Dress Down Anyday'. This shows how far work has moved from its old moorings. Work has always been a kind of corset, confining us to specific places at specific times, demanding certain mannerisms and conventions. The focus the Fourth Industrial Revolution has placed on reskilling and trying to outpace automation has often added to the feeling that we humans are bit-part players, acting our roles, wearing our costumes, with little or no agency. But this is now changing.

By dressing in a more casual way, we are showing that the rigidity and formality of work no longer suits us. Rather than power dressing, which dominated working culture for so many years, athleisurewear is about comfort and freedom. The hoodies and leggings that can accommodate a school run or a jog plus a Zoom call are emblematic of a new holistic identity which allows you to be your complete self.

The Stocktake and the Solopreneur

This new freedom in how we work and what we wear to work may appeal to employees but is not popular with everyone. It represents a direct threat to the corporate leadership preference for office-based, business-suited presenteeism, a far simpler model of productivity than the hybrid one that leaders have been compelled to embrace. By the summer of 2021, 70 per cent of business leaders said they expected a blend of remote or hybrid working to be the norm but no one asked them whether they actually liked the idea.[3] The assumption that returning to the office *had to be hybrid* was so widespread it resembled another fashion craze.

Not everyone embraced it: 'After the indulgence of WFH

and comfy clothing I want to be excited to dress up to impress my colleagues and clients; to win business that brings new products and solutions to knotty and entrenched problems,' wrote Jennifer Blainey of Hanover Communications to 150 employees in August 2020. Yet within a year LinkedIn was telling its 16,000 employees globally that they could indefinitely choose to work remotely or in a hybrid fashion. It became increasingly difficult for any self-respecting CEO not to have declared themselves in favour of flexible or part-time work even though in practice it requires a complete change in the way we work. The combination of technology, generational shifts and identity politics plus the pandemic experience of remote working means that the old singular identity of the corporation has shattered.

And it is not just the corporation but the whole way we think about work that needs rethinking. Enlightened executives of large-scale organisations have understood this acutely and responded accordingly. Anoushka Healy, Chief Strategy Officer at News Corporation, a media organisation with 22,000 employees spread mostly between the United States, UK and Australia, and incidentally one of the global businesses which did not rush to announce a hybrid strategy, says of the way the company devises working packages that it is:

> playing into the flexibility that people will need differently across the generations. What someone who is well established in their career needs and how they want to run things for their family can be different from the younger generation, and it's important to differentiate and not to inadvertently make anyone feel that one singular 'new normal' working model prevails. Yet you have to hold at the core what the business need is. This is a moment of stocktake.

Stocktake is a good way to put it. The push for hybrid working and the desire to view work from a more personal standpoint has affected not just employees but also employers, so 'the boss' also has to be a mobile, skilled, socially adept and agile worker now, who can flit across time zones and office spaces, work seamlessly online and in person, and work with their staff to deliver growth. The Nowhere Office brings new identities for all. The old model of the top-down manager has gone and instead their role is far more complex and places considerable cost and burdens on them from property portfolio management to recruitment and training strategies. Hybrid working is neither cheap nor convenient for bosses, and arguably it raises a bigger question about agency: how much do people want to work at all? Just 17 per cent of City workers in London said they wanted to return full time in the summer of 2021 at the same time as a California congressman, Mark Takano, introduced legislation to reduce the working week from forty to thirty-two hours because 'a shorter working week would benefit employers and employees alike'.[4]

This all represents an identity crisis that was set in motion long before the Nowhere Office era. The rise in income and workplace inequality broke into public consciousness during the Co-Working Years with the proliferation of 'zero hours' contracts which allowed mainstream businesses to act as if exploitation were acceptable. Of course, the fundamental foundation on which work is built has never altered: the division between capital and labour. But that doesn't mean people feel comfortable knowing others are suffering. A sense of fairness is very evident and growing. Forty-seven per cent of Americans now own shares in the private companies where they work and 72 per cent say they would prefer to work for an employee-owned organisation.[5] The 'purpose agenda' – the new name for 'corporate social responsibility', which ends 'shareholder primacy' and instead addresses questions specifically around sustainability and climate change, supply chain fairness and equality and diversity in the workplace – is driving everything from consumer tastes to employee expectations.[6] A workplace has to be identified with fairness or it will be identified with the opposite and drive away the 'talent' it wants to recruit and retain.

Yet work continues to matter to people. People need to work and they want to work, even if they need to do so differently. Research in 2021 by the University of Birmingham that analysed a decade of European Working Conditions Surveys found that the overwhelming majority of European workers felt that they *were* doing useful work.[7] As twenty-three-year-old Lewis Wedlock, a gifted young black influencer academic and activist based in Bristol, England, said to me: 'I truly value work. I'm fuelled by passion. Not working isn't part of my identity.'

So work remains vital and often enjoyed despite its manifest stresses and strains – but its identity has undoubtedly changed. At the core of the whole work–identity crisis is the way we perceive ourselves. The Nowhere Office represents an era in which the first few conversational exchanges with a fellow professional no longer focus on 'And what is your job title?' so much as 'Do you work Hybrid?' or 'What are your main tasks?' Identity and status may come not to matter as much as the way you live and work. Everyone in the Nowhere Office is now managing a new career model, one where they have to take responsibility for everything, and if you had to name a single universal worker identity now it would be the 'solopreneur'. While the rise in entrepreneur-led business during the pandemic is striking – McKinsey predicts 'a generation of entrepreneurs' – solopreneur describes a hybrid of employed or subcontracted, freelance, part-time workers, those whose jobs the International Labour Organisation describes as both expanding but insecure.[8] They have to make their own luck. They have to manage their own career security, progression, often with not one client but several – even within the same organisation.

Reclassifying the identity of all workers to a greater or lesser extent not as full-time workers but flexible part-time solo-preneurs is every bit as significant a shift as moving from the factory floor to the office in the first place. But there have also been other significant changes in the way we think about individual identity within the Nowhere Office.

In and Out Groups

It has become the norm to think about identity in terms of gender, sexuality, class and race, both inside the workplace and in the public sphere, reflecting the growing recognition of significant inequality around all these issues and the harmful effect of these inequalities not just on individuals but also on businesses and society more generally. Since the 1980s the rise of the Learning and Development market,[9] including Diversity Training and Unconscious Bias training, grew to $357 billion, which represents an average spend of over USD $1300 for every employee in the world on 'Workplace L&D'. By 2021 'Pride Month' was more or less a corporate cele-bration of LGBTQ with a rainbow superimposed on all the corporation's branding. Yet a culture war is raging inside and outside the office around the separation of sex and gender and a new era of workplace lawsuits are just beginning.[10] Take the 2020 judgement in a UK employment tribunal case – *Taylor v Jaguar Land Rover Ltd* – which ruled that the car company owed an employee £180,000 damages due to 'well-founded' complaints of harassment on account of their gender reassignment.

By the time the pandemic began in 2020 some of this investment in reducing discrimination was paying off in big systemic changes in attitudes at work and better representation on boards.[11] Attempts to address gender inequality, for instance, meant that women were less likely to be compelled to do what a friend of mine did: she was a single parent for years and would either miss her children's school concerts or construct an elaborate reason for being absent from 'office drinks'. Race identity also took centre stage during the first wave of the pandemic, triggered by the death of George Floyd and the rise of Black Lives Matter as a campaigning force, which included a challenge to existing workplace culture in many institutions, not just the police. In the summer of 2021, Dame Vivian Hunt, a senior partner of McKinsey and one of the most prominent black women in business, reposted a quote on LinkedIn by seventeen-year-old Darnella Frazier who filmed the police attack on George Floyd and tagged it with the stark prediction: 'Change come fast and change come slow but change come.' Alicia Garza, co-founder of Black Lives Matter, is right when she says that 'identity politics hold us accountable to ask more questions about for whom progress is being made'.

Fundamental identity issues around race, gender and sexual orientation still urgently need to be addressed at work. But in the Nowhere Office, where the very identity of work itself has been shaken, will individual identity politics matter as much? How will this be voiced when the question of visibility at work will range from in-person to on-screen (where everyone gets the same-sized digital 'office'); where there may be few or no office co-habitees or working norms any more? Rights over flexible working, subsidies to adapt home working spaces, or local tax differentials when old 'offices' disappear and reappear in a new location, will also start to matter and compete for campaigning time. In the Nowhere Office I predict the discussion around identity will increasingly zoom in on this question: *do I or we belong in this workplace* because it suits who we want to be as a group of individuals in a shared endeavour?

Sarah Pinch, a portfolio career woman with her own consultancy who integrates running pro-bono organisations, told me:

When I first set up my business in 2013 we did not have an office. We all work from home and our homes are all around. Having an office never made sense and so in that sense it has not changed. And yet everything changed. No longer were our homes just for concentrating in, we had to juggle partners and children 'at home' too. Some of my black and minority ethnic colleagues have talked to me about the power of the screen – the fact that everyone has the same height, the same prominence and how that enabled them to find their voices. Yet for those who don't have a safe space to work from, quite literally because of home-based constraints, or budget constraints – not everyone can afford the extra heating – it's all been and could continue to be superbly tough. We still don't want an office – but we know now just how much we want to be together. That's our identity now: the Team.

Sanjay Nazerali is the global client and brand president of Dentsu X, the Japanese-owned fastest-growing advertising agency in the world. He explained:

Culture used to be all about the brand – Steve Jobs's minimalist Apple branding, or the colour black being the cool colour. These are reference points but now the culture of how we work, of what comes out of a new collaborative culture of working is what will inform the identity of brands. Talent is the new frontier, and you can create a new identity culture in this new nowhere quite successfully, it turns out.

Unequal Identity

Collaborative identity, according to Sarah and Sanjay, is the next big thing. And I don't doubt it. Yet the politics of power and identity are never far away in the new world of hybrid working. As Sir Vince Cable, former UK business secretary, put it:

> Hybrid working is unquestionably reinforcing the dividing line between the new labour aristocracy of professionals and senior managers and the proletariat of 'necessary' workers, digitally challenged and others lacking educational certificates and contacts. The world is becoming more divided with the labour aristocracy working harder and more enthusiastically because creativity and the exercise of authority are satisfying, and others are working harder because they have to.

The British journalist Suzanne Moore, who writes 'fully remote' for different media, was clear that worker identity in the end is about the power to make your own choices:

> I'm OK, I have choices because as a commentator I could take my identity elsewhere, and work from anywhere. But my eldest daughter, she's pretty much been told: back to

the office five days now. Not everybody is going for this hybrid thing. It doesn't matter how you see yourself, it's the job. If you're told you've got to be back there's not going to be a lot of say in it, really.[12]

It is certainly true that jobs are precarious and challenged. The World Economic Forum's assessment that automation and what it calls 'the Covid-19 recession' is causing 'a double disruption' is a rather understated way of saying that to work at all is to experience great change, pressure and stress.[13]

Despite the apparent flexibility and freedoms, many inequalities remain and too many people still have to work too hard and too long, despite all the changes in how and where we work. No one has yet come up with an alternative economic model which allows us to work substantially less. So in the meantime, how best to classify the new identities in a meaningful way for the times? This brings us back to the idea of 'hybrid haves' and 'hybrid have-nots', which I wrote about in the Introduction. They matter more now, arguably, than former classifications about 'white collar' or 'blue collar'. I believe we need new labels to capture the essence of what working in the Nowhere Office is really about.

Learners, Leavers and Leaders

In addition to the hybrid haves and hybrid have-nots and the identity of the solopreneur, there are three new groups which arguably matter most in the Nowhere Office because they locate a person within their stage of life and their role. They are the Learner, Leaver and Leader: those at the start of their career, those mid or late on in their working life, and those influencing the decisions and daily direction of those who work with and for them. These three identities determine what workers expect to take from office life and – just as importantly – what they should be expected to bring to it.

These groups span the uniquely broad intergenerational cohort active in working life today, from those who were born around 1945 and are ending their careers but are often still working (and thanks to the global pension crisis many either won't or can't retire); the 'boomers' and those they work alongside in Generation X; the digital natives of Generation Y (millennials) and Generation Z.[14] In under a decade they will be joined by the Alphas, those currently still in school but approaching the age of sixteen when they can be counted as belonging to the workforce. Never before has there been such a diverse workforce with such different needs and expectations. The historian Eliza Filby put it to me like this:

Generational identity aside, we are also ageing differently in the twenty-first century. We are in education longer, living in the parental home longer, meeting partners and having babies later. The traditional ways of incentivising workers – i.e. status, pay and security – no longer work with younger generations because they are prioritising different things. Nor does it work with older workers either. Rising individualism since the 1980s has precipitated a shift from loyalty to the firm to loyalty to yourself and your individual path. Purpose and fulfilment at work has become the ultimate goal.

The Learner

The Learner is typically a Generation Z arriving at the workplace, for whom the importance of location and proximity to other people in order to absorb intelligence, subtle cues, and benefit from their experience, is greatest. This generation wants the best of both worlds: freedom and a place in an office they can visit at times of their choosing. Esther Akpov, a British-Nigerian twenty-one-year-old fashion, culture and tech influencer, embodies a Learner's approach to work:

> I am currently working remotely as a community manager for a creative hub part time, two days a week. Most of the team work remotely. I prefer it as it's very flexible, especially as I am still studying at university full time. We use tools such as Slack to maintain communication and Trello for project management, as well as our own in-house portal. I work and study from home. As a Gen Zer, my ultimate goal is to be a digital nomad. Remote working gives me freedom to travel, explore as well as save time and money making trips to the office.

Learners want the freedom to work remotely when it suits them, but also to enjoy the benefit of going into the office for social reasons and possibly for creature comforts too. Often the showers are better, the coffee is better than they have at home, and it is free. The Learner may be well educated and have passed through many hurdles to get their job – increasingly it's an assault course being interviewed multiple times by Zoom – but they are not well paid and knowing little of work itself they need to be around older, more experienced workers as much as they need to be stimulated socially.

Another Learner I talked to is the millennial advertising executive Rose Eccleshare, thirty-two, who started a new job during Covid-19 and never met her colleagues for a year, connecting entirely with them online:

> The actual work itself is probably easier to get done on your own. I'm much more efficient. But for me, it's that

ten minutes after a meeting in an actual room with actual people. Essentially all of your anxiety dissipates because it's part of someone else's problem as well. Whereas if you have a bad meeting on Zoom, or a good meeting, you just hang up, and you're like, oh my gosh, OK, what just happened? What do I need to do? What were the outtakes? There's no feedback.[15]

What will matter to Rose's career progression is the ability to acquire all of the skills and experience she needs to perform her job. If she is only in the office 20 to 30 per cent of the time, it will be much more difficult for her to acquire all the informal knowledge – the 'birdsong' – that comes from an impromptu chat at the coffee machine or simply by watching other more experienced people and imitating their behaviour.

Anxiety about the loss to Learners of vital social capital – the skills to build networks, to watch and learn in ways that cannot be quantified by qualifications earned – was repeatedly mentioned by older office workers in their conversations with me. David Shriver, communications director at global tech retailer Ocado with 15,000 employees who has built a stellar office-based career over several decades, said:

> What Covid has shown us, I think, is that social capital degrades a lot faster than we think. A hybrid model embracing work from home and work from office is fine, but we all need to recognise that social capital is a lot harder to build over Zoom and that there is a cost to neglecting it.

This was echoed by Helen Brocklebank, CEO of British luxury trade body Walpole, who has embraced Nowhere Office life yet notices this of younger team members:

As we rebuild the culture of collaborative working and creativity we will retain a flexible working day measured by productivity and output rather than a rigid 9.30 to 5.30 . . . 'learning by seeing' becomes so much harder – the access to learning from the talent and experience and example of more experienced colleagues is more diffuse.

The veteran British economist Hamish McRae, seventy-seven, also vividly made the case for learning through seeing:

When I went to the same office day in and day out, I was just watching people work. And not just watching people work, it was actually watching older people socialise and interact with other people. Someone would say to me 'I've got to have lunch with so and so, you'd better come along, you can ask the clever questions.' And I'd notice I'd learn by just seeing the way the interaction took place. You can't do that online.[16]

Of paramount importance to Learners is the ability to learn by trial and error. Learners don't know everything – they do not have the experience. So they need two things to develop their skills: firstly, excellent teaching and mentoring as described. And secondly something else entirely: the ability to fail. The bestselling management writer Charles Handy was until his fifties a career man in Shell. He went through his Learner years and came out the other side:

We were opening a new petrol station in Kuching, the capital of Sarawak, Malaysia, where I was based. As I drove to work, past this service station, which they were going to open later that day, I saw that the huge drum that holds all the gasoline had popped up in the middle of the forecourt. Because the town was on a riverbank and the water table was quite high . . . we obviously hadn't put enough weight on top of the tank. This was a minor disaster but luckily the sales manager wasn't coming for another week, so we managed to push it down, put enough cement on top of it and it was beautiful by the time the sales manager arrived. And the photograph was taken with him and me standing there, on this perfect, perfect new service station. If you can hide away and make a mistake and correct it before anybody notices, the learning is much better, because you're not punished for it.[17]

So the Learner needs to be given the opportunity to pick up skills and signals. They need to make mistakes and correct them on their own with little intervention (and perhaps watch how their elders don't make such mistakes in the first place). They want freedom but crucially they need to be around older people, around the Leavers, in order to be reassured, to face any failure without brooding on it (alone or imagining they have failed when in fact they may be doing just fine), as Rose expressed so well.

The Leaver

The Leaver requires as much flexibility as possible to reinvent their career. They are likely to be a Generation X, a boomer, or a millennial with young children and may well be juggling personal career development with caring responsibilities at home. They are unlikely to be retiring so much as reframing and reorganising what they do. Flexibility matters a great deal to them, so the Nowhere Office may be well suited to their needs. Their sense of purpose is shifting in line with new dependencies, but also new priorities. They may have notched up several decades in 'corporate life', and successfully reinvented themselves as freelancers or flexible workers to better manage everything they have to juggle. Until 2019 there was a dramatic rise in the number of Leavers who became freelancers, the most visible kind of solopreneur. Data from 2019 shows that the top five freelance fields are writing, customer services, administration, data entry and education and training, and that the average freelancer is a female Generation Xer (born between 1965 and 1980) working in the creative industries.[18]

Surprisingly, despite the increase in the number of Leavers who are freelancers, they have a mixed approach to office life. Some are attracted to the stability of office life, having spent the larger part of their careers in it. According to Jacqueline Nettl, an HR adviser to central government working in London:

> We do not operate a hot-desk system for all staff and this is appreciated. There is sufficient space for all employees to have their own workspaces, along with extra stations for temporary hires and visitors. Most staff like 'their' workspaces and feel some attachment to them. This tends to be the case more for older people of course. The age balance in my organisation is weighted towards the over forties, with a significant number of over fifties and sixties.

Yet others relish the freedom of not having a fixed desk for the first time in their careers. Gaby Darbyshire, the Los Angeles-based CEO of digital media company QXR Studios, told me:

> We want to work in person and are finding ways to get together soon, but we are geographically distributed and we likely won't ever get an office space. All of us are fine

on Zoom because we are older. We've built our reputations and our networks.

Most Leavers have mastered the technology required to work, communicate and collaborate remotely without too much difficulty and it is a largely positive experience for them as it allows them the flexibility to manage the cross-generational demands made on them – caring for children, and for elderly parents. In some ways the Nowhere Office could have been designed for them – with one caveat: they risk being citizens of nowhere, losing the social support and social capital that comes with work. When in previous eras they might have been approaching the pinnacle of their careers they now find themselves in a world without any hierarchical mountains whatsoever. And this flatland also feels much more empty than the bustling office they have left behind, and into which many of them invested so much social capital. It may be lonely at the top, but it can be much lonelier in the nowhere middle if you wander into it unwittingly.

The Leader

Leaders set the rules. They create the policies and they manage. The concepts of management and leadership long ago became entwined and muddled and the differences between them are best articulated by the late great Peter Drucker who noted that 'Management is doing things right. Leadership is doing the right things.' Either way, many of those whose role is to be an arbiter of rules, regulations, recruitment, training, strategy, direction and implementation have long struggled to fulfil all of these functions.

The Leader has the biggest shift to make in the Nowhere Office. Rigid top-down management models are going to be out of sync in the network environment. It will take exhausting amounts of energy and new systems to command and control as before. For Leaders the change is as much as anything psychological. They will have to learn to *let go*. Youth tends to favour flexibility and the Learner has less responsibility and more freedom – to be a digital nomad, for instance. Such is the anxiety about recruiting and retaining Learners that they are likely to receive a lot of organisational sunlight. The Leaver is in some sense also having their moment in the sun, because the unbundled, unrestricted, reinventing atmosphere of the Nowhere Office favours some aspects of their needs and life-style. But the Leader has to learn new ways of working and managing at a personal level, as well as creating a workable vision of the future for everyone, in a world where everyone else wants as much freedom as possible. The Leader is often a hybrid of either the Learner or the Leaver. This ought to make them sympathetic and attuned to the new demographic but the burden on them managerially is often enormous. Take human resources – often rebranded now as 'people' or 'talent' in an attempt to soften its harsh reputation as being inhumane in its approach to managing employees. Leaders in HR have to deal with vast amounts of complexity. An influential report from 2021 covering 4,000 global HR professionals shows that there are ninety-four separate business capabilities that affect their performance.[19] Frankly, that's too much. The Leader has to simplify what they are expected to do in order to be sufficiently focused.

Good leaders know that excessive busyness is something to address – often starting with themselves. The pandemic has given them pause to re-evaluate. Their life is now closer to the rhythms of those of their colleagues, which should allow them to have a greater instinctive sympathy for the challenges facing their staff as well as the business bottom line.

Culture Club

Most of all Leaders are going to need to represent the kind of culture they want their company to project. This is no easy task, made much harder by hybrid work patterns and scattered workforces. It is Peter Drucker, prophetic again, who reminds us why culture creation is a supreme business priority in one of his most celebrated quotes: 'culture eats strategy for breakfast'.

Brittany Forsyth, former head of HR at Shopify, an online business which grew quickly into a $7-billion commercial giant, gave an interview in which she said:

> Determine what behaviours and beliefs you value as a company, and have everyone live true to them. These behaviours and beliefs should be so essential to your core, that you don't even think of it as culture.[20]

But you need cohesion and continuity to create a culture, the very things upended by the Nowhere Office's fragmentation. Work has to find different ways to provide a sense of culture, of community, of identity; it is essential to generate loyalty, and to secure the commitment of those employees who might otherwise move job at the drop of a hat. As Jennifer Blainey of Hanover put it in a 2020 memo to staff: 'You're not just an Office, you're a living organism that creates and fosters identities, culture and brings together people from different backgrounds.'

Until the Nowhere Office and the evolution of the hybrid workplace the system dominated the employee. The job title prevailed. Worker identities mushroomed, as a reflection of the wider culture but perhaps also as a way of asserting control in an environment largely outside of most people's control. Now an enormous amount of choice and flexibility is suddenly available and working identity is shifting into simplified focus: are you a hybrid have or hybrid have-not, and are you a Learner, Leaver or Leader?

3

Shift 3: The Productivity Puzzle

Where I stood in relation to the means of production and the rest was a blank to me. Nowhere, I preferred to think.

Ian McEwan, *Machines Like Me*

Mondays you're still fresh from the weekend. Wednesday you already look forward to Friday. But Tuesdays . . . Tuesdays are No Man's Land.

Shirley Hazzard, 'Official Life'

Picture the scene: a windswept beach in Normandy, northern France. Not ideal conditions for a modern Nowhere Office – there are warmer places to tap on a laptop from – but this wasn't a modern Nowhere Office, although arguably it was a prototype for it. The site of the back office of the D-Day Normandy landings had no access to the internet (which had not yet been invented) nor did it have sofas, breakout rooms or breakfast bars. Yet it existed physically on that windy beach. There were desks and filing cabinets and machines. Team spirit, hard graft and results: it all came together on that drizzly sand. When Martha Gellhorn reported on the D-Day landings in June 1944 for *Collier's Weekly* she was awed by both the human suffering and the productivity. 'It seemed an incredible feat of planning . . . Everyone was violently busy on that crowded, dangerous shore.'[1]

Behind the operations of British and Commonwealth and American forces on the beaches known as Gold, Juno, Sword, Utah and Omaha was a back-end operation that has been largely hidden from history. It is a riveting example of what can be achieved with great planning and organisation and is probably the last example before Covid-19 of an epic logistical move from fixed to transient arrangements. In many ways it was a blueprint for today's Nowhere Office and its newly nomadic nature of operations formed through adversity.

This Nowhere Office was constructed with six supply unit headquarters, twenty-five Base Supply Depots, eighty-three Detail Issue Depots, complete with banks of IBM tabulating machines to record information on punched cards. While the troops fought for freedom these units kept supplies running and information flowing. Every detail of this is immaculately recorded – as befits any bureaucracy – in an A3 volume bound in gentle grey cloth called *The Administrative History of the Operations of 21 Army Group on the Continent of Europe 6 June 1944–8 May 1945.*[2] D-Day's operational office was a form of pop-up, a re-creation of old arrangements in a new and temporary location. In adjusting to an epic threat, it swept away all the old inefficiencies which incrementally build up around bureaucracy. The dry understated language of the account is vividly and oddly riveting: 'Considering the size and nature of the operation, the number of typewriters lost or damaged beyond repair during the assault, or by subsequent enemy action, was surprisingly small.'

The remnants of D-Day's back office are literally now grains of sand. The only record of it ever having physically existed to organise a reserve of over eight million rations of food (enough to last fifteen days) is in this magnificent and moving clothbound book with its 151 pages and 25 appendices including hand-drawn illustrations of 'Main Depots in the

Advance Base' through to the mobile office records themselves – the schedules of 'periodical jobs' and 'Hollerith ad hoc jobs'. It hums with a sense of both purpose and productivity.

The office of D-Day proved of course that the office is not so much a place as a system. A series of functions, uniting in a common cause to produce something: victory, success, results, products. The gritty reality of productivity, from war to commerce, is facilitated by the office. You can be productive anywhere now, given the right tools and the right motivation. But what of the common purpose? This is the third shift of the Nowhere Office, the impact this moment is having on both raw productivity and the more nuanced issue of 'purpose' itself.

The Pitch of Frenzy

It is notoriously hard to quantify productivity, hence the way economists refer to the 'productivity puzzle'. Clearly what counts as productive in a call centre is different to measuring the outcome of creativity in an advertising agency. The inherent time delay between the start of a project and its completion is often where the problem of being able to measure meaningfully what is 'productive' lies. I'm thinking for instance of the gap between someone writing a legal or policy paper and its eventual outcome in court or in a new law. It is not as linear as judging how many words a minute can be typed or essays marked in an hour.

The simplest way to judge productivity is personal – does output (physical or intellectual) correspond to someone's needs – and professional, is it aligned with the organisation's needs?

The hope is that hybrid working will usher in such flexible, work–life balance friendly policies that productivity will go up. It is too soon to tell if the effect of working from home or in a hybrid arrangement has been positive, negative or whether it is dependent on other factors that might affect the Nowhere Office. Data shows that worker satisfaction can positively impact productivity by as much as 12 per cent and having the choice to work flexibly is clearly what office workers want.[3] But the picture on productivity in the Nowhere Office is not clear yet. For instance, the Becker Friedman Institute at the University of Chicago looked in detail at 10,000 IT workers who changed to working from home, and it showed that overall productivity actually dropped by 20 per cent.[4] Research from Microsoft presents a picture it describes as evidence of 'high productivity masking an exhausted workforce': 40 billion more emails were sent during lockdowns, for example, and all metrics of digital use related to working from home are rising as sharply.[5] That said, Nicholas Bloom and his colleagues at Stanford reported in their paper 'Why Working from Home Will Stick' that workers surveyed report 'being more efficient working from home during Covid than they were on business premises before Covid'.[6]

Long Speed

Before the current Nowhere Office placeless, timeless environment, managers often relied on old guard rails to measure productivity, such as presenteeism. Simultaneously productivity levels globally have been stagnant for years. This stagnation is in marked contrast to the way the world is speeding up generally. The urban jargon for something annoying or aggravating is revealing: it is the word 'long'. Consumers are sold speed as convenience, as edge, and we are impatient if our screens do not load superfast or we have to wait for online orders which would have taken days or weeks in the past. By contrast, office life and bureaucracies are notoriously sluggish while workers feel under increasing pressure to be more productive. Productivity (and indeed profitability) is closely linked to people's well-being. A key study published in the *International Journal of Productivity and Performance Management* concludes:

> As expected, increased stress leads to reduced productivity and increased satisfaction leads to increased productivity. When work begins to overlap with workers' personal lives this implies a negative effect on productivity. Quality work is more related to conscientiousness and personal satisfaction than workload. Energetic and active individuals affect productivity positively.[7]

Upton Sinclair's 1906 famous novel *The Jungle*, about a meat-packing factory, became a classic for articulating the stress loaded on manual workers. 'If we are the greatest nation the sun ever shone upon it would seem to be mainly because we have been able to goad our wage-earners to this pitch of frenzy', he wrote. Over a hundred years later the Nowhere Office is bringing to the fore the issue that even the professions have begun to feel themselves at a pitch of frenzy working intolerably hard and many of them quite clearly no longer want to be as violently busy in the future.

In response to the pressure of modern work there has been a trend which is not just anti stress but pro extreme relaxation. Luo Huazhong, a millennial factory worker from China sparked a movement called 'Lying Flat' in which the *raison d'être* of life is flipped from being about working hard under stress to doing as little as possible.[8] Millennial rejection of old working norms is also seen in bestselling books such as *My Year of Rest and Relaxation* by Ottessa Moshfegh, which depicts work as largely pointless. In this novel the twentysomething protagonist decides to lie flat for a year and withdraw completely from society. She takes to sleeping in the closet of the art gallery where she is supposed to work. The novel became a bestseller across generations and with good reason. We can all, to some extent, relate to the antihero's feeling that work is not inherently rewarding, that it drains us, and that we'd rather crash out in a cupboard if we could. One global corporate invited me to sit in on a Zoom to discuss the new working landscape and all everyone wanted to talk about was stress and work–life balance. An anonymous user wrote in chat:

> I was in our Montreal office yesterday and it was great. My boss was in as well and I had a really good opportunity to have the hallway chats. My stress came in the morning routine which I had forgotten about – getting the dog walked, kids fed, finding pants, and then the actual commute . . . Similarly coming home, wanting to be back for bedtime and not being sure if I would be, so needing to leave the office a bit earlier than I would have liked, worrying how that might look.

Vitality v Bullshit

Against a background in which work is experienced as demanding, stressful and consistently fails to deliver a sense of purpose, a growing body of books has appeared echoing widespread frustration with the status quo and demanding more purpose and meaning and even simply less work. The psychoanalyst Josh Cohen's 2018 *Not Working: Why We Have to Stop*, a lyrical exploration of work's impact on our psyche, is one example, in which he writes: 'We are witness today to an investment in the conception of the human being as above all, and in all senses, a *working* being.' I'd put Josh Cohen in an emergent purist camp which believes that work represents a failure of society, certainly of capitalism, and that work is essentially not an opportunity but a threat: 'The reason I didn't pursue a career in law, accountancy, finance, corporate management, the civil service or any other respectable middle-class profession . . . was that they all seemed to assume a belief in work as its own justification.'[9]

This view became more widespread during the Co-Working Years, peaking perhaps as we entered the Nowhere Office in 2020 with anthropologist James Suzman's book *Work* in which he speaks of 'avariciousness amplified' and argued that the growth mindset of big business was not only disastrous ecologically but morally and emotionally.[10] The title of Sarah Jaffe's 2021 book says it all: *Work Won't Love You Back*. Again, as in other areas, Covid-19 was accelerating a pre-existing trend. Take sociologist David Graeber's highly influential 2018 book *Bullshit Jobs*, which built on an essay he'd written five years earlier, arguing that it is political control of the workers by the owners of capital/business which ensures that the shorter working shifts, which technology was supposed to usher in, constantly elude most workers, and as a result so too does a life of more meaning. The issue is surely this: how can you be productive in any job if it holds no meaning and is poorly or unfairly managed?

A nuanced view of 'bullshit jobs' was developed by the philosopher Hannah Arendt in 1958 when she argued that through the *vita activa* of work, labour and action, we engage with the world, and our lives have meaning which is determined by who we are as workers. She wrote in *The Human Condition*: 'Society is the form in which the fact of mutual dependence for the sake of life and nothing else assumes public significance and where the activities connected with sheer survival are permitted to appear in public.'

Arendt believed that the human condition is fundamentally linked to our being workers, albeit with distinctions between production and labour, with no suggestion that this would or could be otherwise. I agree; I believe we should work, need to work, for reasons above and beyond purely financial ones, though those are real enough too. To work is *not* pointless. Or it does not have to be. Yet professionals were certainly sold work as exciting and full of meaning. Not exactly mis-selling but overselling.

Purpose-Driven

It is not hard to find fault with the modern workplace. Much of it is shorn of fairness, of meaning, of value to all but a few at the top. Much of it is poorly managed. The very phrase 'toxic workplace' tracks back to the 1980s, during the Mezzanine Years when there was increasing political turbulence in the workplace amid the competing pressures of rising globalisation. At one extreme, the Silicon Valley phrase 'zero drag hiring' began circulating in the Co-Working Years and conjures up the venal vulgarity of capitalism unchecked: workers who had no lives outside work, no responsibilities other than to the corporation were regarded as more desirable than those who had home-based responsibilities and wanted to work in a balanced way.

On the other hand, inequality rose up the political agenda, as did the idea of stakeholder capitalism and its impact on climate change, sourcing, fairness and equality. By 2019, 200 of the world's top corporations announced a new commitment to going beyond pure profit in the Business Roundtable.[11] This new sensibility was echoed by a major project funded by the British Academy, one of the more august bodies furthering research in the humanities and social sciences, called 'Future of the Corporation', which, it ambitiously claimed, 'lies at the heart of the future of capitalism, the future of humanity and the future of our planet'.[12] Purpose had replaced corporate social responsibility as the byword for a more inclusive and mindful response to what workers and consumers want.

Purpose has become, to echo Gloria Steinem's feminist rallying cry of the 1970s, both personal and political. It is a starker moment of transformation of our attitudes to work than we've seen since the Optimism Years, which frames the beginning of this period of work. Rather than being marked by formal industrial action, strikes or campaigns led by unions, it is organic, atomised and individual. The purpose agenda is obviously political in the way it affects how organisations behave and their responses to big issues such as climate, equality and diversity, which are judged not just by employees but also by the wider public and media. How companies and their sense of purpose measure up in this new world is reflected against very public benchmarks such as the Fortune 500 most popular companies. Click on the corporate website of Walmart, the largest company by revenue in the world, and number one in the Fortune 500, and you find a dedicated webpage to 'Global Responsibility: using our strength to make a difference' with copy straight out of the new purpose playbook: 'We believe that our work is not only beneficial for our business bottom line, but also creates shared value for customers and society.'[13]

Generation Z's arrival in the workplace brought a set of social expectations that their older colleagues, even if they shared them, had failed to place centre stage. They are three times more likely to say that the purpose of business is 'to service communities & society' rather than simply sell products.[14] Yet their elders are not that far behind: 64 per cent of US adults now think that the primary purpose of a company should be 'making the world a better place'.[15] Over and above the values an organisation projects to external stakeholders, and how much it walks the walk on the 'shared value' side, it now also has to square things morally with the 'personal purpose' of its people – employees and freelancers. Purpose drives productivity on all sorts of levels. Some research puts purpose-driven companies outperforming the stock market by 42 per cent.[16] People are less productive if they don't think the company they work for is purposeful and they start to move away from organisations whose values don't align with theirs.

Corporations are most at risk from a withdrawal of labour, which we can see in the increasingly frantic efforts of big companies to attract workers back after the pandemic with perks, and the increase in people leaving the corporate sector to become entrepreneurs. Nick Jones is founder of Soho House, the private members' club with 100,000 members around the world and now a thriving workspace business, Soho Works. I've known him for twenty-five years during which he has built a global empire around the more glamorous creative industries in some of the most competitive cities in the world: London, New York, Istanbul, Berlin. He has office space in the middle of one of his clubs in London a stone's throw from the London Eye. He talks constantly to members and observed:

> I've noticed a distinct change in our members. They used to work for big brands, many still do, but increasingly they don't want to work for corporations; they are more entrepreneurial and they want to work for themselves but they've also lost that blind faith that corporations give them the same values. They prefer to work in small teams, create

their own purpose and meaning. As a result of course, where and how they work will change too.

His view chimes with that of Bruce Daisley, Twitter's former MD in Europe who is now an author, podcaster and consultant on the future of work. He believes that the shift to the employee is fundamental:

> I'm seeing a significant sign of worker mobilisation. Overall workers are not going to accept what is laid out to them by bosses unless it fits with what feels right to them. And there'll be two mechanisms on that. On the one hand vocalising concerns and becoming non-compliant. Like Apple experiencing the pushback on their decree that people need to come in three specific days a week without sufficient consultation.[17] And this impacts the second mechanism which is market effect. There are some organisations who have just made their decision and said to me, 'we're going to have people back to the office four days a week'. Well, they aren't desirable employers any more. It's a bit like a salary policy at football clubs: suddenly your policy isn't competitive. Take some of the big investment firms which were for five days a week in the office: as they start losing people and they're trying to attract new workers, they're going be presented with this challenge. Do we pay 30 to 40 per cent more to have people in five days a week? Because that will be the only way to attract them, not just saying take it or leave it. Because people will say: 'I'll leave it.'

This desire for a sense of purpose and recognition that workers are not just parts of a machine but have full lives outside work isn't, by the way, confined to the cappuccino class of high-tech, high-salary, high-maintenance workers in the creative and brand-led industries. Bruce advises every kind of organisation from local government to old industrial businesses pivoting to digital. He and I both sat for several years on the board of the Workforce Institute, and I remember our reaction to a particular presentation for a board away day at IKEA's global HQ, back in 2017. One of the managers said they were pivoting to a more flexible schedule based on what worked best for the lives of their people and for the first time they were trying wherever possible to allow shift workers to request that school concerts or caring responsibilities were accommodated. For an office coordinating 445 retail outlets around the world serviced by nearly 220,000 employees changing the system was no small management undertaking or cost. Bruce and I looked at each other and I could sense we both just thought: Wow. This is a moment of change. This isn't bosses telling workers what to do so much as workers telling managers 'This is what works for us', and managers having to rethink and refit the patterns of work.

The Third Person in the Room

Can technology drive productivity or will it further enslave us to more pointless presenteeism (of the digital kind)? Ever since Klaus Schwab of the World Economic Forum declared the 'Fourth Industrial Revolution' in 2016 the upper echelons of management and leadership have had to contend not just with redressing inequalities at work or the rising pressures (and rewards) of globalised commerce, but also with the competition their own workforces face from technology's relentless march forward. The World Economic Forum's latest prediction is that by 2025 machines will do more tasks than humans.[18] Some of those lost jobs will be recreated elsewhere but undoubtedly the Nowhere Office ushers in a third machine age in which we will share desk space with robots sooner than we think. Hybrid working patterns plus the rise of VR mean that we will increasingly collaborate and work with colleagues in a virtual way – Meta's announcement of Horizon Workrooms, using its Occulus Quest 2 VR headset, marks a new phase in virtual meeting and heralds an acceleration of a trend which had to some degree been put on hold during the years of frantic flying, conferences and in-person meetings.[19]

Right now many people are clinging on to the belief that we will snap back into the kind of working life dominated by in-person presenteeism and meetings – but I would not bet on it. Why? Because people care about their own productivity. They not only don't want to work at a stressful pitch more than they have to, but they want to do so *productively*. This explains Zoom's success. Let us not forget that while Zoom had been around for a decade before 2020, it was seen as a second-best option, one forced on remote workers by necessity and distinctly less powerful than being in the room. Now, despite its many failings, people are recognising that used in the right way, teleconferencing can open up new possibilities that had been overlooked before. Finella Craig, consultant in Paediatric Palliative Medicine at Great Ormond Street Hospital where she supervises the care of very ill and dying children and babies, had an epiphany during the pandemic when it came to using technology:

The office at the hospital always used to be my base but now? It's a rota. Most of the time I write my management plans and take calls from my bedroom. I do video calls with families. I don't feel I've lost anything. I feel I've gained. Obviously if children are coming to hospital seriously ill, travelling, especially during Covid-19, is not a good idea. We just never used video because it wasn't 'done' but now that seems such a strange decision. I always offer a visit, but by video it can be quicker. For instance, the other evening a family were worried about a child's breathing. I got on the video and watched and was able to diagnose then and there. And also there is an equality: when I do a home visit I'm going into their personal space. On video they also get to invade mine! It makes a connection. But really, the saving on travel time means more time as a team together, also on video. It's been transformative. Not at all negative. And this surprised me.

Finella and her colleagues had to break with a culture that saw remote consultations as negative and build a new culture where they could be seen as beneficial in certain circumstances. They also found that working remotely didn't diminish the social aspects of being in a team, but enhanced them. With the time saved on travelling she was able to start a book club with colleagues and a Friday-night Zoom cocktail hour, which they could never have done before.

Then I spoke to Professor Barbara Kellerman, James MacGregor Burns Lecturer in Public Leadership at Harvard University's John F. Kennedy School of Government, who also found that technology was not nearly as stressful as she had been led to believe:

Every time I'd open my email, I'd see yet another instruction to be aware of how teaching online is incredibly different from teaching in person. And I can only tell you that in my case I found that essentially what worked live in the classroom worked quite well. My own finding was that what works well in person tends to work well virtually.

The expectation was that it wouldn't, but in practice guess what? It did.

So it is clear that old-style offices and presenteeism are not the only way to foster productivity or even a sense of being present. Quality and motivation matter – driven and productive people who care about what they do. And technology, the third person in the room, can help with this more than we ever imagined possible. Sanjay Nazerali of Dentsu X told me that:

> What I've found is that a very intense and profound culture is created amongst teams collaborating digitally, despite concerns to the contrary. When you're working on a global pitch, with perhaps thirty to forty people spread out across the globe and the different disciplines, we're using a whole bunch of different platforms – Slack, Teams, Zoom – and it creates relationships which are profound and deep. We get to know each other very well, even when we have never met face to face. Yet the purpose of what we're doing is enhanced by, enabled by, culturally enriched by these platforms, they don't detract from it.

Sanjay's point is instructive, because he emphasises both that productivity itself can be creative, but that technology is a driver of it. A by-product of digital collaboration may also minimise the toxic culture of office politics, which in itself is often a drain on energy, time, focus and productivity.

But, of course, the caveat is this: the technology has to work and keep working. Too often it glitches and then a distributed workforce in multiple locations cannot be productive at all. The spectre of a system going down is never far away. Take the six-hour outage of Meta and its apps in October 2021 caused by a maintenance error. The number of people on Facebook is 3.5 billion – higher than the total number of workers in the world – so the impact on those working on this 'social media' forum was considerable. Our social selves and our work selves are inexorably linked now.

The tech we use going forwards has to be the tech we trust, or the whole of the Nowhere Office will teeter on its foundations. The reliability of technology, and its resilience against either cyber-attack or basic human error remains a big 'what if?' Temporary pandemic lockdowns will feel like nothing if the digital lights go down for any extended period of time.

Fully Present

There's a famous saying that 80 per cent of success is just showing up.[20] The Nowhere Office affects presenteeism quite literally, and one productivity boost is the ability of organisations to hire people across a far wider geographical area than was thought possible or desirable pre-pandemic. But there is a more psychological interpretation to the idea of presence, too.

Being present, physically but also in terms of mindset, having focus, is crucial to productivity. We are all familiar with the problem of zoning out on Zoom, tuning out instead of staying attentive. As the management guru Adam Grant wrote: 'I've found that productive people don't agonise about which desire to pursue. They go after both simultaneously, gravitating toward projects that are personally interesting and socially meaningful.'[21]

So there it is again, the link between purpose and productivity. The first thing to figure out is what makes you feel, or your team feel, *there*, metaphorically as much as physically. Louise Chester, who trains and teaches thousands of the world's top corporate leaders in leadership with the consultancy Mindfulness at Work, says:

> I've noticed increases in a sense of purpose in leaders. This manifests as a strong desire to do what is meaningful, systemically impactful and value-creating and not dissipating energy or wasting valuable time. They too have realised that a life well-lived doesn't happen when we're looking the other way, and that in order to live that life we need to get really intentional. Productivity is very connected to being able to continuously focus on and connect with the right people and priorities – a core function of mindfulness is being centred and having what we call presence, precisely because it leads to productivity. Distraction, the constant pull of judging whether data is salient or not, disconnects us from the bigger picture and pulls us into the weeds of reactivity and tactics, closing us down neurologically to the bigger picture and sustainable long-term goals as well as the ability to have the aha! moments or insights to harness the potential latent in the present.

What I find interesting about Louise's perspective is it's a much tougher take on mindfulness than the more touchy-feely kind which has begun to prevail. She links purpose to productivity through what she calls 'presence'.

What about the other kind of presence – the 80 per cent of showing up? Bruce Daisley is right that no matter how much executive pushback there is in some quarters the zeitgeist has changed:

> Most of us sat in the office, answering emails quickly before we went to our next meeting. It was nothing like the version

that we've created in our heads. And I think, for a lot of people, that distance will become vividly felt when you're on the 7.22 into London, thinking, Man, I had a year or two not dealing with this. All sorts of companies, from iconic modern ones to old industrial model turned digital businesses are now busy writing the first draft of the new version of history. Because business has been found wanting, where they now recognise that the way they were working before wasn't fully functional. The way that they've worked in the last twelve months has been remarkably adaptable in the face of huge changes. But you know that they've considered that unsustainable. And so they're looking with an open mind thinking, well, how can we set about creating a new version that is focused on succeeding in all the ways that failed before?

Pattern Management

One risk of hybrid working is that it opens up so much possibility that there are no rules or systems at all and it hinders rather than aids productivity. Some form of standardisation is necessary even if it is much more short-term and iterative than before. But I believe the groups I identified in the last chapter – Learners, Leavers and Leaders – will all find their own rhythms of work, even if there is no one size fits all in any industry or sector. For years large geographic businesses like Walmart have had a daily check-in call. Fully remote business leaders routinely do this with their teams. The internet company GoDaddy is fully remote but has always had immersive three-day gatherings of teams at regular intervals. One company uses Instagram Stories to post about working lives so people can stay connected.

However we do it, in the hybrid world we will need to manage our own time – those stubborn, un-stretchable 168 hours in the week which we humans need a third of to sleep through and another third to do things like get ourselves or a child dressed, put on a kettle, clean a bathroom or pay our bills. Time is going to be judged and measured differently now, less so in seconds and minutes and hours but by tasks which we match to our environment. Quiet time to do Cal Newport's famous *Deep Work* concentration. Or time to collaborate, brainstorm, exchange information in a loose way someone described to me as 'random collision'. Or time for our private lives with the implicit agreement of managers and leaders about what success looks like professionally – leaving us to decide how to allocate the time we need to achieve this. All of this will need to be explored and consulted over, workplace by workplace. All of which will need new patterns, standardised or customised, to reflect both the values and what is most productive for those involved. These choices around time and task will become as familiar as the difference between a carbohydrate and a calorie – different ways to count outcomes.

At the end of his book *A World Without Work*, Daniel Susskind warned of 'the problem of meaning, of figuring out how not just to live with less work but to live well'.[22] Productivity is going to become more, not less, visible in the Nowhere Office. It will be obvious if people are working well, and it is obvious that they will exercise their choice in line with personal purpose and corporate purpose. The age of being violently busy is all but over.

4

Shift 4: New Networks

I don't feel I've had a good day unless I've talked with at least one new person. We have a meeting, make space for new people to come in. The organizer sits next to the new guy, so everybody has to take the new guy as an equal. You do that a couple of times and the guy's got strength enough to become part of the group.

Bill Talcott quoted in Studs Terkel, Working

Even bonobos, one of our closest primate ancestors, will open a trapdoor in order to share their food with strangers as long as there's a little social interaction first . . .

Susan Pinker, The Village Effect

Networks are the lifeblood of professional and personal relationships and taking a fresh approach to them is the fourth big shift in the Nowhere Office. As the world of office work becomes increasingly hybrid, nomadic and freelance, those with strong networks will fare better than those with weak ones. Managers and leaders who recognise the dynamics of the social science of networks will create better working environments than those who do not.

Serendipity will need to be manufactured in the Nowhere Office. Internal networking won't happen as easily as it did when you could walk into a bank of elevators and bump into someone from another department, or past a row of desks and stop for a chat. As I have argued in Chapter 1, face-to-face contact gives an advantage which cannot be replicated as precisely over Zoom or in chat rooms. The office will remain a great place to network and that may become the USP of the office over anywhere else.

This chapter looks at five particular aspects of networks and networking: social capital; proximity and distance; diversity; networking online; and why institutionalising networking as the core function of Nowhere Office life is a smart leadership move.

From Golf to Stilettos

Networking and building connections have always been integral parts of doing business. Back in the Optimism Years the rigid hierarchy, racism and sexism of the top-down office made networking simple but exclusive. Promotions in a straight, white, male-dominated workplace came from the golf-course circuit, excluded women and ignored anyone who did not fit a certain archetype. During the Mezzanine Years the office was a deskbound place, without laptops, internet or mobile, and women were still a long way from having parity, often excluded by their caring responsibilities from the after-work drinks and the informal networks which drove promotion. It was only at the beginning of the next working phase, the Co-Working Years, that government and corporate awareness of the significance of networks began to rise and a widespread shift began. Two particular academic papers published played a role. One by Herminia Ibarra and Mark Lee Hunter in the *Harvard Business Review* in 2007 entitled 'How Leaders Create and Use Networks' and a year later Nicholas Christakis and

James Fowler's paper 'Dynamic Spread of Happiness in a Large Social Network' brought an understanding of network science to a wider public and specifically gave a modern context for the science of sociometry pioneered by Jacob Moreno in the 1930s and the famous 'six degrees of separation' social network analysis of Stanley Milgram back in the 1950s.[1] These papers made it clear that networks were positive tools for improving not just working environments but society at large.

Contemporary networking began to have its moment. This coincided with a growing awareness of social inequality and a focus on social capital. The idea of social capital has been around for centuries but was first defined as a theoretical concept by Bourdieu in the 1970s, and what happens to people when they lose it was famously explored in Robert Putnam's book *Bowling Alone* (2000).[2] It has steadily picked up credence and supporting data in policy circles ever since.

Networks are intrinsic to social capital because of what Robert Putnam articulated as the 'social networks and the norms of reciprocity and trustworthiness that arise from them'. Two kinds of network began to thrive as people needed them to both 'level up' politically but also as the white-collar job market became increasingly competitive and insecure as a result of globalisation. On the one hand there were support networks based around identity focusing on disability, gender or sexual orientation, and on the other social networks often industry-led which focused more on areas of special interest or skill. Pamela Ryckman's book *Stiletto Network* and Sheryl Sandberg's *Lean In*, both published in 2013, drew on both kinds of network, and contributed to the movements that produced political gains in the boardroom and indeed the rise of #metoo. These networks directly challenged inequality and led to a more meritocratic social approach. Such was their success that networks were more widely appreciated as more people began to experience their benefits.[3] The Co-Working Years were also marked by a huge upswing in conferences and a study of professional women across America in 2018 showed that women's chances of promotion doubled if they belonged to certain conference circuits and networks.[4] LinkedIn, the pre-eminent social network for professionals with 750 million members, began to take off in 2006, on the cusp of this period.[5] It launched as a platform to showcase and circulate your professional CV. Suddenly social networks legitimised in-person networks and vice versa.

The Rebirth of Distance

As the Nowhere Office era began in 2020 a new networking era dawned. During lockdowns WhatsApp group usage soared by 40 per cent as isolated professionals realised that for all of its faults the office provided some kind of in-built network structure they had to remake alone.[6] The management writer Frances Cairncross famously described the internet era as 'the death of distance'[7] but the Nowhere Office sees its rebirth. It is widely acknowledged among recruiters that the pandemic has widened the talent pool substantially.[8] As I wrote in Chapter 1, everyone is more #GenMobile than they were before. Yet people crave close connection and they find workarounds when they cannot do so in person. Social networks are in many ways perfectly suited for the times because they are a blend of the personal and professional. The disclaimer on many a Twitter feed that the writer is 'writing in a personal capacity' sounds tissue-thin. The person tweeting and posting personally is the same as the professional, and everyone knows it. Personal networks benefit or hinder professional networks, and vice versa, they are inextricably connected.

The global online events market is due to grow by 23 per cent by 2028 as travel budgets remain curtailed and health fears linger, and the psychological shadow of Covid lasts.[9] Although in-person networking has a particular salience because it builds trust and intimacy, it is unlikely that the tradition of vast conference arenas packed out with delegates seeking a mix of talks, inspiration, booth-browsing, and freebie pens and candy will return at scale. Informa, the world's biggest live professional events business, reported a 42 per cent drop in its revenues in 2020. When people do return to professional networking gatherings, I predict they will lean towards smaller clusters, more like salons, and that much of what they do will be hybrid: live streaming at scale was pioneered by TED Talks when their own conferences grew too big. In Nowhere Office times, instead of expensive time and travel budgets people will favour in-person gatherings for far more focused and special purposes, reserving larger networking to be done digitally out of their newly refurbished offices, or in local hotel suites, co-working spaces or indeed their living rooms. Sophisticated new digital social networks such as Hopin, which came into the marketplace during the pandemic, are likely to be used more, not less.

Highly Peripheral People

Networks succeed if they are able to remove the distance between people and nurture a degree of trust between them. Physical proximity often favours influence. There is a famous YouTube video of a man dancing in a field in the Sasquatch! Music Festival in 2009, which is regularly shown at leadership conferences because within minutes he has influenced an entire group sitting on the grass around him to join in. A network can emerge from almost anywhere, but it must emerge from somewhere – a cocktail party, a chance encounter at the elevator or in the airport lounge. Conversations that might appear to be marginal can end up being vital: the periphery can often be as important as the centre. Network science is all about the distance between hubs and nodes, and for people a famous study by the sociologist Mark Granovetter in 1973 entitled 'The Strength of Weak Ties' showed that the informal, peripheral connections such as a social introduction rather than formal job application were often more successful.[10]

During one of the several long lockdowns I bumped into Rohan Candappa, a British writer and director with Sri Lankan heritage, in our local park. He told me he had consciously been doing something previously unthinkable: building his networks.

Last year would have been the 40th anniversary of us leaving school so there was going to be a big reunion, but because of the pandemic that didn't happen. But because of the pandemic I had a Zoom account so I thought I'd get my money's worth out of it and just set up loads of meetings to try getting in touch with people, and others got in touch, so we ended up with forty people on a Zoom call, some of whom I hadn't seen for forty years. It struck me that it was quite important to be in touch with other peripheral people. They don't have to be people you already know are important in your life . . . having peripheral conversations gives you different angles and points of view and helps get you out of the spiral of your own head. Different people and different experiences matter if you're open to them. We've begun to realise networking isn't transactional or venal. I would have felt allergic to the description of being a networker; I saw it as meaning furthering a career. In advertising I never really networked as I should have done, networking as a term or concept wasn't what I was drawn to but now I understand it differently. It's much gentler than I had realised, and much more rewarding.

There is another dimension to the periphery. The organisational network analysis (ONA) expert Rob Cross coined the memorable phrase 'highly peripheral people' to describe the hidden assets of knowledge and insight tucked away inside organisations. Referring to those in whom 'untapped expertise and underutilized resource resides' Cross found they were often far from the corner office.[11] Harnessing the knowledge and connections of a network of workers who are often and intermittently far from each other geographically is a critical challenge for leaders. Bringing people in from the periphery and hearing their contributions regardless of their job titles or status will become vital as organisations inevitably flatten. It might even be said that the network approach will end the silo structure, which is the bane of organisational life because at the heart of great networks is one thing above all: diversity.

The Diversity Dividend

Rob Cross conducted another piece of research in summer 2021 which gave an interesting insight into the ways different groups network. He looked at diverse communities within ten different organisations. He found that Asian males had very good networking skills, which were reflected in their promotions and advancement, while black women and Latin American men fared considerably worse.[12] This demonstrates that networking is partly attitudinal, partly cultural, and a lot to do with opportunity. You have to be in the right kind of job to be able to network – and then you need the confidence to do it. Interestingly the development of the virtual office and the use of Zoom in particular has broadened networking opportunities for some black and minority ethnic groups. People who felt underrepresented and unheard in the physical office benefited from the equality of everyone being the same size on screen, with none of the rigid hierarchies of the conference room table.

This point was echoed by the digital entrepreneur and investor Tom Adeyoola who told me:

I met more people during Covid-19 lockdowns than I would have done in the physical world. I attended start-up pitches in Northern Ireland, Cardiff, the north of England. I mentored founders in Jamaica, South Africa, the Commonwealth and all around the country. I would never have been able to do that before the pandemic unlocked the visual medium as a norm. This should be a fantastic moment to proactively break people out of non-diverse 'mirrortocracy' networks to improve diversity and inclusion and spread social capital.

This is why the campaign for greater diversity in corporate and public life links to our understanding of networks and specifically social capital. Who we know and what we know helps us get on in life and in our careers.[13] The basics of network science apply universally. The larger a network, the more opportunity there is. The stronger the ties within one network to another, the higher the chance of 'spread' – of ideas, opportunity, connections.[14]

Networks need to be structurally diverse, cross-sectional and span different disciplines, ages, class, race, gender to generate what has become known as the diversity dividend or the diversity bonus. This refers to the tangible benefits, not just moral but practical and financial, of having a diverse empowered workforce. Businesses and teams that include a range of different kinds of thinkers from different backgrounds systematically outperform more homogenous groups in terms of innovation. One study by Boston Consulting Group saw that corporations with above-average levels of diversity in their management team achieved 19 per cent higher revenue.[15] A large study of 1,800 people and forty companies by innovation experts Sylvia Ann Hewlett, Melinda Marshall and Laura Sherbin discovered that those with greater diversity were 45 per cent more likely to report growing market share and 70 per cent capture of new markets.[16] Plainly, diversity works at work.

The opposite of diversity is a limiting and ultimately stultifying groupthink. It creates mono-mentality, the kind that led disastrously to the sub-prime mortgage crisis or the cover-ups and silent acceptance of the culture which resulted in #MeToo. When everyone is either hired in the same image, or comes from the same social groups, healthy networks do not develop. Worse, they shrink. Not allowing for dissent, for different expertise and opinion, is not only immoral but tremendously costly too.

Organisations should start to mix up the formations of in-house networks and make them more like office parties – where everyone gets to mingle regardless of age or rank. This is not to say that specialist networks should be dismantled, but that a new emphasis should be placed by leaders on what the network science shows, namely that diversity should show up right across the board, starting with company networks themselves.

The Collective Bargain

As the Nowhere Office develops there is one gap in the structure and management of networks within the workplace that has to be addressed if social capital and diversity are to expand and not shrink. The workplace has been very good at siloed, special-interest networks, reflecting the importance people attach to seeing themselves and their communities represented. But the slimmer, simpler demographics of Learner, Leaver and Leader that I identified in chapter 2 need some kind of unifying force, a network to represent each of them. You might think that ideally trade unions would fill this gap. Studs Terkel's union organiser Bill Talcott, quoted at the top of this chapter, reflects the utopia of *belonging*, which unions in theory provide: 'Our society is so structured that everybody is supposed to be selfish as hell and screw the other guy . . . we are trying to link up people, binding them together in some kind of larger thing.'

But trade union membership has been declining globally for years. There are many reasons for this but one that is often overlooked is that unions too have neglected to capitalise on the value of building networks or teaching their members how to network better. Yet each demographic of generational workers – Learners, Leavers and Leaders – has significant potential to belong to new configurations of networks, and if trade unions were seen as an enabler of networking this could be attractive. Of the Generation Z Learners I talked to it is significant that they belong enthusiastically to numerous networks yet none belongs to a trade union.

Take Bejay Mulenga, the award-winning social and digital entrepreneur who by the time he was twenty-six years old was running both not-for-profit foodbanks and highly profitable corporate consulting enterprises:

I'm not really aligned with a lot of trade unions. I don't come across them. I do know they are very important, but I've always felt that if you are a young arrival or even a middle manager you join the back of the queue, not the centre of the conversation immediately. They have been valuable for many years, in lobbying and moving the needle forward on equality but I think there's been a creation of a lot more task forces, working groups, not actual networks.

Mulenga emphasised that the problem with unions wasn't just that new arrivals felt at the bottom of the ladder, but that the very long-established rhythms and protocols of unions felt slow, cumbersome, and unable to react quickly to fast-changing issues that mattered:

There are already formed formalised ways of working. It's not happening in real-time, it's about monthly meetings. It's slow. It's not giving voice. It's single issue. I am not saying that the trade union is dead. They will have to modernise. No network can exist off social media or just meet quarterly or monthly with a traditional board.

Interestingly, it is not clear whether trade unions are confident that they can appeal to the next generation: a European study in 2019 found that a fifth of young people in work had never joined a trade union because they had not been asked (and another fifth admitted they had been asked but had not got round to it).[17]

Most trade unions are currently concerning themselves with the collective bargaining challenge of drawing up contracts for workers who need new protections around working from home, in terms of cost and safety and campaigning. But campaigning is not networking. It can actually be alienating for some people who do not regard themselves as political but who do want to feel they gain something from belonging to a network. Unions could address this gap. If they were to position themselves as brokers of social capital or vital knowledge between organisations and their workers, they might reverse their decline in the Nowhere Office.

The Long Lunch

The shift from a place and task-based working culture to one focused around people will require both new networks and new confidence to go out and network. An IBM survey famously found that high performing organisations were 57 per cent more likely to invest in collaboration and social networking.[18] Organisations wishing to equip their hybrid workforces for the new working environment would be wise to increase the investment they make in allowing their employees time and budget to develop contacts. The global restaurant business lost $240 billion in revenue during the pandemic; allowing more working lunches will be a smart investment as well as a boost to the economies of cities and suburbs alike.[19]

The idea of the long lunch, or the liquid lunch, to oil the wheels of a deal is rooted in the intrinsically social aspect of hospitality with another person. Networks work best with trust and intimacy. Breaking bread or being social around food and drink is an incredibly fast way to achieve trust. Eating together may be the biggest single network advantage someone can have compared with connecting purely online.

I talked about this with the social philosopher Charles Handy. His 1994 book *The Empty Raincoat* first identified 'the portfolio life', which arguably anticipated the Nowhere Office. In the summer of 2021 he predicted this:

Organisations are going to be like a gentlemen's club in Pall Mall. Which, if you think about it, only members are allowed in and once you're in, there are lots of offices, but they don't have the name of a person. They have the name of a function. In other words, for reading, for eating and so on. And so lots of people want to work like that. They want privacy but they want immediate access to other people and I think the wise organisations will have a sort of club annexe, the main feature of which will be the dining room. And they'll probably offer free breakfasts and free suppers to allow people to congregate, but then separate out into their other work.[20]

I broadly agree. The place you network in is going to resemble less a siloed single-use building than a space redesigned for social use *first*, with at-desk work a distinct second.

Offices need to be redesigned and repurposed not just to attract workers back (and install or upgrade vigorous ventilation to do so safely) but in a way that also recognises the need to improve offices that are not well designed for networks. Tom Adeyoola thinks that office networking was a benign accident, not a carefully constructed design:

I think the office always used to be effectively a lazy construct that allowed serendipitous events to happen within the office environment helping networks happen in an almost semi-autonomous way. That's fine. Now as hybrid takes hold we will need to deliberately structure management and the connectivity that happens to bring everything and everyone together constructively.

The requirement to bring people together to give them purpose and cohesion is real. Brooke Masters, noted this presciently in the *Financial Times* in early 2021:

97

Many of the youngest workers have never met their bosses in person. Juniors feel less connected to the institution, and seniors find it hard to judge when underlings are struggling. That's one reason why many are pushing to get people back to the office.[21]

Kevin Ellis of PwC echoed the point Brooke Masters made. He believes that if you're not in the room you might be missing out on serious social glue and savvy you can't replicate easily in any other setting, especially when it comes to conflict resolution. As he said to me:

> There's no doubt that personal relationships through being in the same room are at their most important in times of tension and trouble. So I might know a colleague in Japan, or France or America pretty well and have met them, formed a relationship. But the next generation might only know them through the remote filter of the screen. And when you've got a problem, now, will you be able to reach out with the same result?

Ellis believes that there is a significant risk that 'the class of 2020/2021' will suffer career-wise if they cannot catch up on the important face-to-face connections which act, to use network science parlance, as 'brokerage and closure'.[22]

The Network Navigator

If this kind of networking is so important yet difficult to recreate in the Nowhere Office perhaps employing a chief network officer is a logical next step. There is a role at a practical level for hearing people's views, noticing reticence and building confidence, resilience and inclusion. Organisations that organise check-in meetings for teams build trust and networks, as well as capturing vital information that may be at the periphery but needs to come into focus at the centre. Elizabeth Katz, vice president for risk management and corporate compliance at a large health-care system in Lancaster, Pennsylvania, coordinates what she calls 'the daily huddle':

So we have a lot of different organisation-wide efforts around communication and continuous improvement; you can't do continuous improvement without communication. Our teams huddle every single day, virtually, and they talk about the same things every day – patient harm, infrastructure issues, staffing issues, employee patient harm. So it's a very constructive way to talk on a daily basis to troubleshoot and resolve problems. The problem-solving happens at the staffing level. Those issues go up to the management level, then it goes up to leadership, executive leadership level, so there's networking from the bottom to the top. We call our system 'Safety Net'.

In oncology there is a role called the 'nurse navigator' who joins up the process for a patient on their painful and frightening journey through treatment. Any patient with a chronic serious condition knows that you enter a world of uncertainty and complexity. Often there are layered consultations, meetings, venues, all of which require joining up. That is what the nurse navigator does. The Nowhere Office needs a navigator too, someone senior like Elizabeth Katz, to connect disparate opinions and draw the threads together.

This is because in a placeless world, in a world without the usual signage, we need to create new navigation systems, new roles. Being worried about fitting in and needing help onboarding is one kind of networking need. Being listened to when you have a great idea or want to push back on a deadline for good reason is a different kind again. New networks, new measurements and new navigations: it's all much more possible, not less, in the Nowhere Office.

So the challenge for leaders is to reconfigure their workspaces to prioritise social engagement, while promoting take-up of digital social networks in a way that is productive and builds corporate cohesion. The old model of scaled networking (conferences) or no networking is unlikely to remain viable. Instead, we will see a new centre-stage role for networks in the Nowhere Office, possibly with traditional trade unions playing catch-up, and most certainly a mash-up of in-person and digital interactions. We will experience a more diverse way of deploying people's experiences, perspectives and lifestyles, which drives social capital and embodies the true meaning of diversity.

But networks have a built-in fragility: they are connected to and therefore dependent on others. If one link is weak it can be a problem. And more than anything one organisational role needs to be strong: the Manager.

5

Shift 5: Marzipan Management

Almost nothing was more annoying than having our wasted
time wasted on something not worth wasting it on.
Joshua Ferris, Then We Came to the End

Organisations need to find out what their employees want,
rather than making them fit around corporate strategy.
Amanda Goodall, Financial Times[1]

Regardless of the kind of office worked in – from a hospital
to a corporate HQ, everyone suffers from marzipan management. That feeling of being stuck under someone else's orders,
on someone else's timeframe, at the mercy of someone else's
poor management.

The term 'marzipan layer', first coined at the end of the
Mezzanine Years in 2003 to describe the senior managers stuck
one rung below the top leadership in heavily hierarchical
organisations, is apt and applicable more widely.[2] These
so-called marzipan managers impede decision-making and
delay change. Despite the vast budget dedicated to leadership
development ($400 billion is spent annually), the question of
how to unstick bad practices and initiate new ones to take
advantage of the new hybrid world and the hunger for purpose-
based practices remains unsolved.[3]

This matters more and more in the impatient and intolerant,

purpose-conscious mindset of modern workers in the Nowhere Office. This is a moment when all those millions of dollars spent on 'agile' management need to come into their own. The question is, can they?

In *No Hard Feelings* Liz Fosslien and Mollie West Duffy use cartoons to devastating effect: one image, entitled 'Criticism Crime Scene' shows five labelled objects: '(i) Poorly timed critique (ii) Overly blunt delivery (iii) Unfiltered verbal spray (iv) Cutting Remark and (v) Devastated Recipient'.[4] I can relate.

Yet this chapter is optimistic that the fixed, sticky attitudes many of us have as a result of suffering poor managers can and will shift. How? By shifting the focus to two key areas: resetting management systems and prioritising trust. The last twenty-five years of management systems, especially in HR, have increasingly relied on putting digital distance between people and their managers and some of this will need to be reversed to counter the effects of increasingly remote workforces. Trust will take centre stage as the Nowhere Office compels managers to shift responsibility and promote self-management. The rise of the freelance market and the solo-preneur identity will also necessitate this shift.

Powershift

The Nowhere Office is full of wide gulfs between the haves and have-nots: those with true flexibility and hybrid choice and those with little or none; those who can work in a way neither demeaning nor too demanding; and those for whom the status symbol and structure of their jobs require ultra-presenteeism and bucketloads of stress, regardless of how chichi the offices on offer. But nothing is as demeaning or demanding as being badly managed, and nothing is as challenging as managing well.

This chapter is not going to dance on the head of a pin and try to separate 'management' out from 'leadership'. They are to all intents and purposes the same. If you are on the receiving end of orders from someone let's call them 'management'. If anything this chapter is about what Barbara Kellerman calls 'followership'. Those who enable or perpetuate poor practice are the villains here. As she noted in her book *Bad Leadership*, 'It's past time for students of leadership to resist the dominant model – the leader-centred model – and embrace a more holistic one. Leaders should be looked at *only* in tandem with their followers.'[5]

This sensible advice is never heeded often enough. Every corporate scandal features followers who enable bad leaders. This is as true of the Wirecard insolvency scandal of 2019 in which a $1-billion fraud was exposed by a whistleblower at the Munich-based payment firm; or the Greensill Capital lobbying scandal of 2020 which engulfed the reputation of former Prime Minister David Cameron.[6] It seems as if corporations are often not good at practising what they preach and acting on 'lessons learned'. Of course, plenty do, but the question is whether the greater exposure which the Nowhere Office has brought about simply by upending all the old systems and throwing some sunlight on them can make lasting change.

The Nowhere Office marks an inflexion point in which management systems that are cumbersome and top-heavy can be refreshed and created anew. This point was made clearly by Martin Sorrell: 'We're a new company and we started with a clean sheet of paper. Digital transformation is about change management, so as Hubert Joly, former CEO of Best Buy, said, "Change the management."'

Most managers don't intend to be bad and many are simply hapless. And there is perhaps no better example of this than Ricky Gervais's hopelessly unself-aware manager in the TV series *The Office*. Yet the consequences of poor management are far from comic and are played out in two ways. Firstly, in organisational failure, and secondly in the rising figures of stress in the workplace and the widespread revolt against returning to the office. The 2021 Gallup State of the Global Workplace report states in real terms 80 per cent of people 'are not engaged or actively disengaged at work', clearly demonstrating the failure of existing management structures and leadership to provide the support and systems workers need to operate effectively.[7] As the WHO noted in 2020:

> Stress occurs in a wide range of work circumstances but is often made worse when employees feel they have little support from supervisors and colleagues, as well as little control over work processes. There is often confusion between pressure or challenge and stress, and sometimes this is used to excuse bad management practice.[8]

Stopping poor practice requires taking a stand but the marzipan management system often frustrates this. Powerlessness is passed on, creating a vicious cycle of inertia and inaction. But something is shifting – and that is the locus of power itself. Over the past three phases of work, control has started to slip away from management. In response management first of all loaded up their professionals with so much work and so much system complexity – including highly complex pay incentive systems – that they could not really stop to stocktake, object or take any action. Then managers began to use technology to put distance between them and people they were managing. Partly this was to cope with scale and speed. But it also revealed an increasing disassociation which put them out of sync with the times. Lockdowns broke that chain. People now want fairness across society and that includes inside their own workplaces.

Humans are not machines. Technology should enable better communication between humans, not inhibit it. The result has been a collapse in trust which has to be rebuilt urgently.

A recent annual Edelman Trust Barometer shows that half of employees say they are: 'more likely now than a year ago to voice my objections to management or engage in workplace protest'.[9] What that means is something very fundamental: a more confrontational attitude. Workers definitely want more autonomy. Large scale studies, including one from the University of Birmingham, show that autonomy matters hugely to people but is denied to almost everyone except managers, who enjoy 90 per cent autonomy.[10]

This imbalance is unsustainable in an environment where so much work will be done offsite, requiring a significant degree of autonomy whether managers like it or not. Then there is the old way of taking control: voting with your feet. Remember, in the Great Resignation, that one in two workers say they will move jobs within a year in the Nowhere Office.[11] Staff turnover is up significantly and one of the big winners are the headhunters. Why? Because the shift to using the power of networks creates more job opportunities that bypass the current dependence on employers. But above all, the shift is about values and employee expectations. All of which means that the system has to get unsticky to survive.

Keep it Simple

Office work is not straightforward. It requires (among other things) the ability to multitask, the ability to work in teams and on your own, and to cope with different time zones. The scope for misunderstanding, miscommunication and mismanagement is immense. So too is the complexity of the structures that have developed around office work and have grown exponentially ever since the internet arrived. These structures, which have emerged to keep capitalism intact, satisfy customers and stakeholders, as well as cope with the constant glare of the social media gaze, are arguably out of control. But the new schedules and team configurations that hybrid working demands offer an opportunity to rethink these structures and make things simpler.

Simplicity itself is a valuable and proven strategic tool:[12] General Electric's famous 'Speed, simplicity, self-confidence' strategy; the KISS principle in the US Navy (which stood for 'Keep It Simple, Stupid'); Steve Jobs's maxim that with simplicity 'you can move mountains' are all evidence that while we have to respect the complexity of the human, the systems to support us at work need to be *as simple and straightforward as possible*.[13]

The first step is to acknowledge the sheer complexity engulfing the way management and leadership is expected to operate. William Eccleshare, worldwide chairman of media giant Clear Channel International, said:

I think one of the things that the pandemic has thrown up is that organisations grow more complex without you realising it. Because every executive tends to want to have their own organisation, their own power structure. And so as soon as you bring in a new role, you create a whole multiplicity of additional structures and layers in the organisation. And you don't realise it's happening. I think I was surprised how many organisational layers we had created in a multimarket, multifunctional organisation, twenty-nine geographies, the number of different product lines that we sell, and all of the corporate governance that comes with being a public company. All of those things together just made the organisation much harder to control than perhaps I had realised. What we've done is try very consciously to reduce the number of organisational levels that there are.

We habitually declutter our homes and embrace simplicity in our personal lives. The market for mindfulness apps is growing at 40 per cent per annum and expected to reach $4,000 million plus by 2027.[14] As individuals we recognise the value of 'less is more' so it's time to put it into practice at work. To tackle complexity adequately you have to deal with scale. And go small not big. A huge dataset on innovation shows that if you want to change and disrupt, the overwhelming evidence is that a large team will be less incisive and slower to identify what needs to change than a smaller, nimbler one. Scale clutters, smallness simplifies. Professors Dashun Wang of Kellogg School of Management and Professor J. A. Adams, founder of the Computational Social Science program at the University of Chicago, analysed 65 million academic papers published between 1954 and 2015 – i.e. three of the four workshifts covered in this book – and found that 'large teams excel at solving problems, but it is small teams that are more likely to come up with new problems for their more sizable counterparts to solve.'[15] This is a hugely important finding: it not only makes the argument that delayering and simplifying may reveal solutions but the use of the word 'problems' is especially revealing. Smaller, simpler teams see problems better.

It makes sense to simplify systems when so much management energy will need to go into fresh challenges: scheduling hybrid working, reframing the measuring of performance. Many organisations are using daily check-ins with their team on Zoom or Microsoft Teams or Google Hangouts to cut through complexity and just ask each other: how is it going? Sometimes the old systems are the best.

But sometimes old systems themselves need clarifying and reducing. None more so than the one which is front line in managing the workforce overall: HR.

Human Remains

Ask any Generation Z what it is like to apply for a job these days. They will tell you that they spend hours applying for hundreds of jobs online, filling out endless tests and applications which are seldom even acknowledged. Everything is automated and there is little human contact. This is not what applying for a job should be like and it doesn't get much better once you have secured a position.

This complaint sourced from a couple of clicks online is typical of how many feel about HR, not for nothing sometimes dubbed 'human remains' behind its back:

> The thing is, I don't think you start out hating HR. I think I took HR for granted when everything was going smoothly. It wasn't until I had a horrible HR person that I became leery. At my last job, the HR manager was totally incompetent. Morale was horrible, management was worse, and our turnover rate should have been an embarrassment to her. Instead of addressing the actual problems in real ways, her answer was to plan potlucks, send flowery emails, and basically ignore the elephant in the room. She singlehandedly ruined my HR experience. That said, if I ever re-enter the workforce as an employee, I will never take a good HR manager for granted again.[16]

Of course if you look for superstars of contemporary people management there are plenty: Patty McCord spent fourteen years at Netflix and transformed the global standard for innovative practice; Melanie Collins, chief people officer at Dropbox; Nickle LaMoreaux, chief human resources officer at IBM; are all examples of trendsetters. Sarah Willett, chief people officer at bricks-and-mortar warehouse retail business Very, which has transformed itself into a digital retailer embracing hybrid in a highly intelligent way sums up her collegiate approach as 'team of individuals'. Innovation is there and does exist.

And it is important to acknowledge that management and HR are on the front line dealing with the challenges that have arisen from Covid-19.

But HR is the public face of management. And if, as I have established, management needs a dramatic overhaul in order to cope with the challenges of hybrid working, HR is at the front of the queue of what needs reforming. There is no doubt that in many cases the HR department has dramatically failed to live up to what it was intended to be, a fair way to manage the social being who works, has feelings and needs. In the Optimism Years the department was known as 'Personnel'. It focused on labour relations and the unions, the practicalities rather than the emotional state of an office floor.[17] During the Mezzanine Years the American-led term 'human resources' entered the lexicon and with it came industrial psychology, organisational management and the idea of personal development. Its focus was on systems and testing and this is when I suggest the rot really set in.

I would argue the main problem is mission creep. Up until the Co-Working Years HR's focus was on straightforward processing of people, payroll, etc. But automation and globalisation changed that. For decades HR has had an ever-increasing remit embracing workplace culture and values, as well as trad-itional recruitment, training and people management. Treating workers in a really human way in fast-paced, complex and large organisations has become increasingly haphazard and the mushrooming of policies has prevented meaningful personal-isation of employees. If you are essentially hired by algorithm, paid by automation, appraised by an algorithm-led system, where is the personal side of your personnel management? HR is the undernourished, bullied child of the C-suite. HR managers are all too often there to do their bosses' bidding. So in practice the HR department has become part of the problem, not the answer. Emma Jacobs, a *Financial Times* commentator, described HR to me as:

> A big baggy department, trying to do too many things which other managers offload on to it, and it also has reputational baggage: HR is generally the last place that you would go to if you actually had a problem, if you were being harassed, or wanted to change something about how you work. People do not want to report bad practice to HR and just see HR as being on the side of the bosses. That said, I think the pandemic has really put a spotlight on the HR department, and in some places it has really risen to the challenge. It has borne the brunt of considerable changes, which aren't going away any time soon, so the problem isn't the people in the system so much as the system itself. The fundamental problem over the pandemic has been workload and work intensity. No HR department can take that workload away. Only managers can.

Given how technocratic a lot of people management has become – the global HR software market will have grown to $10 billion by 2022[18] – how can it be made more human again?

Possibly the biggest change HR leaders can make is to listen to what people are telling them. Strip away the technological barriers and connect directly. Re-humanise HR. If they can peel away the layers between the leadership systems above them and the real live people working for their organisations, change could be immediate and lasting. In order to do this the current laborious and outdated system of appraisals should be reappraised itself and reformed. The onus should be less on the employee having their performance evaluated and more about the organisation being asked: how are we performing for *you*?

There are plenty of examples of organisations that have scrapped traditional performance management and thrived – such as Brazil's Semco or Sweden's Volvo – which suggests that dropping anything resembling the appraisal is the common-sense approach and a quick win. The generational aspect is important here too – Elizabeth Uviebinené, a Generation Z commentator on work, wrote that 'yearly reviews are hugely outdated. Performance appraisals date back to the First World War. Why are they still plaguing our modern offices?'[19] Quite.

Wear the Shoes

In the end, it comes down to trust. Trust is created when people can put themselves in each other's shoes and find common ground. The problem is that much of management has become adversarial. This may have worked pre-pandemic when everyone was too busy travelling or trying for their bonus or just being too exhausted to notice. It won't work now. This is for one simple reason: emotion. The eminent psychotherapist and social commentator Susie Orbach described the problem to me:

> Work is still not accepted as a legitimate place for what is considered emotionally important or valuable, and you can see this reflected in the systems built around the way people manage other people. Work is a dramatically passionate place for many but it can also be boring and deadening – take emails which just fur up the arteries of professional life. So we have to redraw boundaries, rewrite the systems, for what we really feel and what we need.

The time for top-down edicts is over and leaders need to understand their role in this debate and take a more empathetic approach. Luckily, there are some good role models. Joanna Swash, Group CEO of Moneypenny – a global leader in outsourced communications – thinks:

> We need as a business to deliver great service which is productive, efficient, but with a workforce which feels our systems are built around them as people, not imposed on them because we apply a management method which in itself may no longer be valid. And even if it is for some workplaces it isn't right for ours.

Tellingly, this leader understands something very fundamental: 'We need to put ourselves as leaders into our people's shoes and think how would we want to be treated if it was me?' This was true of all good leaders before hybrid working but is essential now. As Barbara Kellerman emphasised:

> If you're a reasonably good manager in person, the likelihood is that you're going to be a reasonably good

manager with a hybrid workplace. The larger challenge is this: the nature of the relations between leaders and followers, of superiors and subordinates. So whatever conversation we have about hybrid must be embedded in a larger conversation about the issues managers are faced with.

This brings us back to the shift towards talent and away from managers discussed earlier. Mary Appleton of Future Talent Group, an award-winning publishing and learning platform that caters for HR leaders, was blunt with me:

> The rules have been blown out of the water because no longer are organisations bound to certain locations to hire talent, and employees are making their decisions about where they want to work based on a range of issues. The new generation of talent coming in has a new mindset. Whilst I think some organisations acknowledge that it's important, it does not always translate into practical action and practical changes.

This is where my optimism comes in. Marzipan management is in the end a mindset. It is a construct – and it can be deconstructed. The new energy, movement and values of the Nowhere Office will simply demand new models. I was struck early on in the pandemic by something Reggie Van Lee, chief transformation officer of the Carlyle Group said in a digital conference on the future of work convened by Bloomberg: 'Tools are just tools,' he said. What matters is 'what drives productive, inclusive work. The bigger reality is people need to work with others.'[20]

I'd like to suggest a framework that simplifies work structures and releases those marzipan managers from their sticky misery. Leadership and management need to be reorganised around the human at every level and that includes the way we talk about them. SOUL could be a useful acronym, standing for the four things that everyone joining a company has to encounter: Skills; Organisation; Understanding; and last but by no means least, Like. These four elements comprise the technical, managerial, educational and emotional landscape we all work in. We have to constantly redefine and upgrade them. We have to hear and see each other's points of view, learn to disagree, and embrace diversity of outlook and opinion, but also gather together in collective pride and love. Even if we don't like what we do all the time, we have to like it most of the time or what, frankly, is the point?

What would happen if this SOUL mindset became the focus for leadership and management, and everything else was pared back, looked at afresh – just as the floor plate of buildings or the hours of workers are?

While I was writing this book I went to Charles Handy. For many he remains the greatest living management guru and I interviewed him for my podcast about this whole subject.[21] Is there a secret recipe for success today, I asked him, in the Nowhere Office? He replied:

> The good organisation is like a small English village, where everyone knows each other. And you don't have to have job titles or anything: you're just Julia or Charles, we all know what you do, and you all help each other out. And nobody owns the village, you belong to it, but you don't own it. And that's the recipe for a great organisation.

The village is a fascinating metaphor: it includes the idea of ownership – we all have a stake in the ownership or occupancy of our own homes – but it acknowledges that there are many assets that we hold in common. We do not own them – they belong to the community. We participate in, and enjoy, them because we are part of a communal enterprise. The heart of this is trust. We can have difference, disagreement, but not disengagement. And if the village thrives, its commonly held assets will outlast us, as they should. With a new approach to management the Nowhere Office could turn this utopia into a reality.

6

Shift 6: Social Health and Well-being

A state of complete physical, mental and social well-being, not merely the absence of disease or infirmity.

World Health Organisation definition of health, 1948[1]

Autonomy, control, social connections and support foster physical and mental well-being. Any company, in any industry, can pull these levers without breaking the bank.

Jeffrey Pfeffer, *McKinsey Quarterly*, 2018

The rise in sales of the latest office gadget, the treadmill desk, provides a striking metaphor for modern attitudes to work: it is a trudge which can somehow improve our quality of life and even keep us healthy. But does it? The corporate well-being market has grown rapidly. It is worth more than $50 billion, a figure set to rise by 7 per cent by 2028.[2] The catch-all phrase of 'well-being' comprises everything from physical health assessments to mindfulness, amid an ever-increasing focus on mental health. This is because there is a clear causal link between work, stress and the health-related disorders it can trigger. In the United States 40 per cent of job turnover is attributed to stress and for every 47 cents spent on treating depression, it is estimated to cost employers 53 cents on managing the impact of it. In the EU some 60 per cent of all working days lost are attributed to stress.[3]

Never mind 'sick building syndrome' – the world of work has been sick for some time.

Although their work is rarely dangerous or physically demanding, the narrative that professional office workers are somehow privileged and secure compared to other sectors is misplaced. Anxiety is real, and it is rising. Deloitte reported 26 per cent of millennials taking time off for stress and 22 per cent of Generation Z, while the latest data from the US Work Institute's annual Retention Report show that employees quitting their jobs for 'physical, emotional and family-related health issues' has become the second biggest reason after career progression.[4] There are many political and social headwinds that affect stress but conditions at work are key factors. The pandemic has inevitably added to this stress: Microsoft Trends Survey of 160,000 employees around the world found, for instance, that high home-based productivity often masked burnout or 'emotional exhaustion'.[5] All of which paints a gloomy picture of systemic failure. Yet this chapter strikes an optimistic note. Despite the data, I believe the sixth and final shift of the Nowhere Office will be that work *can* be a place where you can truly be 'your best self'.

This will hinge on two things. The first is a commitment to directly addressing the causes of stress at work and righting some wrongs. Less warm words, more action from leaders. This may involve a comprehensive overhaul of the way well-being is articulated and addressed – and this would be welcome. Amending it to 'social health' would be far closer to the mark, as our social selves, the quality of our connection, our relationship to technology, are all primary factors in how we experience work and the workplace.

The second is how to foster community and belonging. Key to this will be a strategy to bring people together for social gatherings and to work harder at creating online community spirit in remote settings. The professional working world is not only going to work less often from offices but less consistently for single employers. In 2019, 59 million people were freelance in the United States compared with 53 million in 2014.[6]

But developing greater community spirit will also require a lessening of the toxic culture wars prevalent inside offices – and they won't abate just because people work remotely (remember social media?). Well-being should work both ways: social health is about social respect. Some of the hostility routinely meted out to employers will need to be dialled down to foster trust, mutual respect and a healthy workplace all round. In other words, well-being needs to be recast, and have operational issues firmly embedded alongside simple, basic human values.

Managing hybrid working at a basic operational level is clearly going to be key to ensuring that office life functions well in the Nowhere Office. Elliot Moss, partner and chief brand officer at the law firm Mishcon de Reya, which has 1,000 people across two offices in London and one in Singapore, explained to me how they are responding with what could be called a well-being strategy:

We need to manage hybrid with great care – it may well favour those with strong social capital so we need to be aware of this and build the capital of those that have less of it. We need to be smart about which meetings are fully digital, and which are in person. Combining the two is very difficult and inevitably leads to a 'them' and 'us'. If by hybrid you also mean WFH vs the office, I think this is less of an issue; 20 per cent of my team have WFH for a decade or so at least one or two days a week. I personally think a change of scenery is excellent for creative thinking, and some tasks benefit from no interruption. So the big pro overall is that the meta-narrative now legit-imises WFH (versus for some it feeling like a naughty habit), and that sometimes being digitally connected is actually a fantastic use of time. The con is that a 2D screen can never give you what 3D life does: emotion, human connection, space and the unexpected. It's not easy to schedule a joke.

Moss neatly encapsulates the themes of this book, namely a recognition that the Nowhere Office is less of a location than *a space* in which, if we want to work together and individually, we need various factors aligned. His comments were not made in the context of well-being specifically, but in terms of the essentials behind productive, high-quality work: getting the work done, with engaged, supported teams. Nonetheless it's significant that Moss highlights a vital aspect of wellness at work: social cohesion and belonging.

Beyond Burnout

But how can the workplace stop being so stressful overall? There is quite a lot of muddle about precisely what poor health walks in the door (metaphorically) with a worker and the degree to which stress is generated by incompetent manage-ment, or by economic and social inequality.

Work should not be a painful experience, to be compensated for with various well-being initiatives but a source of connec-tion, identity, purpose and humanity. It shouldn't matter whether the office is somewhere, anywhere or nowhere; what matters is whether it is a place worth being.

Social Health's Triple Shot

Just before the pandemic the World Health Organisation included burnout in the International Classification of Disease: not as an illness itself, but as a 'factor influencing health status'.[7] It classifies burnout as:

> A syndrome conceptualised as resulting from chronic work-place stress that has not been successfully managed. It is characterised by three dimensions:
> • feelings of energy depletion or exhaustion;
> • increased mental distance from one's job, or feelings of negativism or cynicism related to one's job;
> • and reduced professional efficacy.[8]

It was during the recessions of the late 1970s that the modern idea of 'stress' first entered the workplace lexicon, at around the same time the American psychologist Herbert Freudenberger coined the term 'burnout'. But the concept itself goes further back: Charles Turner Thackray's 1831 paper 'The Effects of Arts, Trades and Professions on Health & Longevity' was a precursor of the literature to come, with Hans Selye's seminal 1956 book *The Stress of Life* triggering an outpouring of psychosocial industrial psychology. However, workplace well-being during the Optimism Years and the Mezzanine Years tended to address specifics ranging from alcohol dependency (a key stress indicator) and workplace safety. Slowly things changed. By 1990 the US federal government launched Healthy People 2000 which enshrined the idea of health being actively promoted within an organisation.[9] The following decade, technology began to control our lives inside and outside work ever more forcefully leading to a different recognition of what being well at work means as the 'always on' culture began to be widespread.

During the Co-Working Years the new focus on well-being came not from medicine, but economics. It was most famously expressed in the influential 2009 Stiglitz-Sen-Fitoussi report 'On the Measurement of Economic Performance and Social Progress'.[10] A crucial section on 'from production to wellbeing' will stand as an important testament to the moment when modern digital society began to reframe its ideas about wellness. That this shift happened not long after the great financial crash of 2008 is not surprising. The growing pressures caused by globalisation, increased automation, and ever more complex management structures, all contributed to making workers feel disconnected from their environment and their sense of purpose and meaning. Greater job and financial insecurity and the pressure to sustain ever higher levels of growth all contributed to levels of work-related stress rocketing and inevitably it took its toll on health and productivity.

My book *Fully Connected: Social Health in an Age of Overload*, published in 2017, put the case for redefining the original 1948 WHO definition of health when 'social well-being' was linked more to class and associated opportunity than to technology. Writing about it for Arianna Huffington's workplace well-being portal Thrive Global, I argued that social health is:

> A successful strategic approach to how we connect with each other in times which are overcrowded with 'infobesity'. The world's soaring stress levels, stagnant productivity figures and cultural drop in trust and confidence in technology and social networks show that there is much work to be done.[11]

I also argued then as I do now that social health strategies at work should mirror the simplicity strategy which underpins a global approach to good physical and mental health. There is a universal focus on just three core elements in physical and mental health: diet/nutrition + exercise + sleep. These three help prevent problems and promote well-being at its core. Everyone is now highly literate about counting carbs and calories, knowing the difference between the benefits of HIIT (high intensity interval training) and the impact of sleep and rest on performance and mental resilience.

What of social health? The elemental trio here is knowledge + networks + time. If you have the right information (including information technology) circulating within an organisation or within your grasp, and a community to turn to, learn from and help, you are more than halfway there. And if you have control over your time, timelines and schedules, this is highly likely to cement a solid sense of well-being.

Social health is about both creating trust and creating conditions which work. No physical body runs well on sugar and saturated fat, lack of exercise or sleep. No organisation or worker can feel properly well if they are pressed for time, lack networks or are disconnected from the information flows they need and deserve.

This is what matters more, frankly, than all the beanbags and mindfulness practice in the world. There needs to be time for face-to-face connection with managers, not just a blizzard of emails and edicts. Loading people up with impossible deadlines or heavy-handed approaches is wrong and ultimately counter-productive. It creates ill will, toxicity, and often a backlash. Research by leadership academic Amanda Goodall clearly links boss competence with well-being, as does McKinsey research which states: 'relationships with management are the top factor in employees' job satisfaction, which in turn is the second most important determinant of employees' overall wellbeing'.[12]

An example of where this can all go horribly wrong is Twitter's appointment of Dantley Davis in 2019 as head of design, which was supposed to shake-up his teams with what the *New York Times* quoted him as saying was 'tough love'.[13] They reported on the effects of this approach:

> Mr Davis, the company's new vice president of design, asked employees to go around the room, complimenting and critiquing one another. Tough criticism would help Twitter improve, he said. The barbs soon flew. Several attendees cried during the two-hour meeting, said three people who were there.

Within a year this approach had been abandoned, but not before Davis himself had suffered extreme abuse on social media and in online forums. You cannot give with one hand and take away with another. Workplaces that want productivity, engagement and innovation have to treat their employees well and not imagine that what might be called bullying in one context is OK because it is cast as constructive. But employees must also behave towards their managers with basic decency even if they resent the power imbalance.

It is clear from the rise in workplace bullying data that well-being is often seen as separate somehow from the actual work handed out by managers, as if it just happens between workers, and never between managers and their subordinates. Recent data from healthcare provider BUPA in the UK showed nearly a doubling of cases of workplace bullying between 2019 and 2020 – to 26 per cent.[14] A quarter of workers not feeling psychologically safe is a troubling number by any metric. How did it come to this? This has to change.

Changing Minds (When the Facts Change)

Given that the pandemic has shown that those who have any choice prefer to keep their stress levels low and work in a way that suits their lives, we need a major strategy change around well-being. Because the fundamental idea that people wish to carry on coming to work and being given well-being programmes is clearly insufficient.

The eminent workplace academic Professor Sir Cary Cooper has spent many years reviewing Employee Assistance Programs (or EAPs) and found that routinely 60 per cent of the stress felt originates at home, with 40 per cent from work. But that also implies that we need to distinguish between real operational stresses – like poor management, working hours or pay and conditions – and personal mental ill health. In the Nowhere Office we have to be clear about the sources of stress or not-wellness in order to identify what measures need to be taken to alleviate them. Nevertheless, once we are 'at' work, whether that is in cyberspace or an actual office with colleagues, the ultimate responsibility for creating a healthy environment lies at the door of directors. As Cary explained to me:

> Covid-19 has forced organisations to dial back on ping-pong tables, massages at your desk, to focus instead on strategy and specifically how you create an organisation where people feel valued, trusted, and you identify the problem areas, and how you correct them.

I then discussed this with Melis Abacıoğlu, founder of the corporate well-being platform Wellbees in Turkey, and asked how prepared for change organisations actually are. The answers were that there are some green shoots emerging:

Most organisations approach well-being as a band-aid tool, because there is no time and no budget – the argument is often there are other more pressing priorities. However, the firms that excel at well-being (and the entire bottom line benefits it represents) do the opposite – they approach well-being as the foundation of the entire employee experience that covers all steps of an employee's journey through the organisation instead of a separate or stand-alone project. They look at what it means across productivity, team management, engagement, or benefits. They see beyond the complexity and focus on what matters: human beings.

So, instead of peripheral fun items – the ping-pong and pool tables – well-being has now arrived as a more central and structural feature. Here is Cary Cooper again:

> Every organisation should have a very senior person in charge of what wellness looks like in terms of policy, behaviour, and a positive impact on productivity will follow that. We now have companies with directors of health and well-being who report to the HR director or the chief medical officer, or in some cases, the CEO. I've spent decades looking at this and finally I think we're on the point of real change.

Despite this optimism (which I share) there are going to be plenty of flashpoints for stress and for the possibility of legal challenges to the way workers' well-being is supported in a hybrid era. The 'right to disconnect' campaign run by the British trade union Prospect is important and interesting.[15] If you are expected to be 'always on' when your home set-up involves shared space, children, poor broadband, bad light, or even just a life which doesn't want to be pinged constantly, and deserves some privacy, these will be rights which need protecting. Not having them is likely to lead to an increased sense of disempowerment, lower productivity and ultimately burnout.

What will work well from Mombasa to Macau, from Minneapolis to Madrid will vary according to the personalised needs of employees and businesses. The one size fits all model has been proven not to work in mainstream health, and it doesn't apply in social health either. Customisation needs to prevail.

Along with a sense of belonging, fairness and equality are essential for workplace well-being. To give just one example, the pandemic has highlighted the way caregivers and working parents experience a double discrimination. Not only must they cope with their usual responsibilities but hybrid working often brings heavy additional pressures such as protecting those who are already vulnerable or home schooling – 62 per cent of working parents surveyed by the American Psychological Association reported higher anxiety than before the pandemic.[16] This isn't entirely new: in 1985 – a time when many women were campaigning fruitlessly for greater flexibility with little support from their male colleagues who generally liked to be in the office or on the golf course – a study of 40,000 women found 62 per cent noted their work was 'somewhat stressful'. So people and times have not changed. Or have they?

Cary Cooper put it like this:

This is an opportunity for a total reset. Of where and how we work; a reset of how we're managed, a reset of location, a reset on mental health, but maybe even a major reset on the role of men in the family. Because I think that is really fundamental. Incidentally, the hybrid model will not work if men migrate back to the central office full time, and leave women to work as they did pre-pandemic on flexible working arrangements, and take on the responsibility of childcare or elder care, as well as working. I don't know whether it has or whether we've created a new man out of this pandemic – time will tell in the hybrid model. Because men's main identity has always been work, the big question is are they now prioritising the family or are we back to the pre-Covid era of divided gender roles?

The Blended Family

Family is a good metaphor for work itself. I believe that the shift to a more successful social health and well-being strategy hinges on cultivating community far more systematically than before. A working life will currently take up at least one third of our lives. The vast majority of us spend as much time with work colleagues as with our own families. In the freelance world of work in the Nowhere Office, workers will belong to several workplace families at once. So a useful model for workplace social health could be the blended family. Organisations are shape-shifting communities of blended units creating both large and smaller families. Multiple-family households provide a great blueprint for new models of resilience, flexibility and understanding. The Nowhere Office with its hybrid-working, multi-generational workforce is like a multi-layered family. In short: workplace social health requires that the office functions like a community, a place where everyone has a sense of belonging, even if the ways and times in which they come together vary as much as the people themselves.

The flexible family of workers will shift across locations and time zones to be with each other. They will behave in one way with one kind of family and differently with others. The free-lance worker will become very much like the stepchild or the child with new siblings. They will adapt and adjust accordingly.

There is a powerful scene in the second series of *Bosch*, the TV series about an LA detective. It is Thanksgiving, and many of the detectives are in the kitchen, wisecracking and arguing as they illustrate that for many of us our co-workers are like our families. We love them, they frustrate us, we may misread and hurt them – just like family. But like family, we would not be without them. Because when we are without family, or a proxy for family with friends or colleagues, we are truly alone.

The Lonely Office

In her 2020 book *The Lonely Century* Noreena Hertz articulates the loss of community that technology can cause and explores the way modern design, despite the best motives, can unin-tentionally create a sense of isolation – even in the open-plan office. Her thesis is backed up by the 2020 Cigna report in which 61 per cent of Americans reported they were lonely at work.[17] The risk of workplace isolation increases exponentially in the Nowhere Office. Atomised WFH models, hybrid and flexible working can all create hidden pockets of isolation where people are not together, despite the Zooms and the tech channels or even the drop-in hybrid days. This brings us back to Elliot Moss's point about jokes: if you have colleagues and people to share jokes with, you are not alone. Not being alone is to be in a social setting. Social health is not only the absence of isolation and the presence of social connections and net-works, but also a flow of information between people that enables them and their work to flourish.

Face-to-face encounters, while costly in terms of time, are

at a premium compared with the widespread broadcast mode we all use digitally. Balancing a sense of belonging through in-person and remote meetings will be key to culture and cohesion. Linda Plant of Edwardian Hotels London said:

> Weighing up the reasons why you need to physically meet someone or consider whether the conversation can be had over Zoom is really important . . . I love physically meeting someone – looking at the whites of the other person's eyes – socially getting a feel for someone and connecting. This can only be done in person because it's tangible. However, I now realise that so many meetings could be done over Zoom without having to race across London. A healthy balance between WFH and WFO – I believe that is what will derive from this pandemic.

What does this mean in practice? Can you create a 'family' out of work and should you? Well, yes and no. The aim here is to avoid creating stress, ill health, poor performance. That is the strategy. If creating a stronger community achieves this, that's a successful social health and well-being strategy, isn't it?

One thought would be to create a secular calendar of specific company-created bonding holidays which favour a hybrid model anyway: coming together less frequently but more meaningfully, and coming together less to do tasks which can be done separately but to do the one thing that cannot be bettered than in-person, namely to socialise.

The Two-Way Street

For too long the idea of well-being at work has been seen as an add-on rather than an essential requirement. Not everyone can love their job all the time, and I'm not even sure I would claim that the concept of 'happiness' is integral to working life, but everyone has the right to work which functions adequately and doesn't cause illness.

Much of the stress caused by work, which triggers physical and mental ill health, can be laid at the door of management. But not all. We all know that it is extremely difficult if your line manager lacks empathy, or the deadlines you are set are pointless, or the software keeps changing faster than your skillset. All of these are factors which affect how *well* you can work. But they should not be confused with your emotional and physical state when you 'go' to work in the first place.

Those who work should be supported if they have physical or mental health obstacles, of course. Most of us will feel anxious or vulnerable at times and some of those times will be at work. Nevertheless, it should be a given that everyone brings their best selves to work, rather than to assume they are going to be somehow short-changed by their workplace or that they are fundamentally prevented from working. If that is the case then their relationship to their workplace obviously needs to be reviewed. In turn the spotlight *must* shine on identifying and eliminating the triggers of stress which emanate specifically *from within* the workplace. That's on the shoulders of leadership. As a manager you cannot be held responsible for what happens outside work but you can be responsible for contributing to an unhealthy workplace in its widest sense – one which exacerbates stress through the presence of impossible deadlines, bad practice, insufficient support, training or flexible working. That is something you, as a manager, can control or contribute to.

A healthy workplace must champion diversity of thought but also not forget that leaders and managers are fallible and may have off days or make the wrong call. They do not need to be hounded for it but treated with the respect, kindness and generosity that everyone is entitled to. This is where the Learner, the Leaver and yes, the Leader should feel the same agenda. The office may be dispersed across geography and hybrid timelines, but everyone needs to recognise that work only works if everyone is in the same boat.

Ultimately, it is about belonging. Belonging to a functional system that creates products and services, in a way that is profitable but which has purpose. Where humans are treated as humans and not machines. Where they feel *seen*. In Samuel Beckett's *Happy Days*, his wretched, gripping 1961 play about estrangement, the character Winnie is buried up to her waist in the first act and passes the time with a series of pointless actions. By the second act she is buried up to her neck but takes comfort in the belief that she matters to someone, even though she is patently completely and utterly alone: 'Strange feeling that someone is looking at me. I am clear, then dim, then gone, then dim again, then clear again, and so on, back and forth, in and out of someone's eye.'

What a metaphor! Work has to function, to have a purpose, or we risk being buried up to our neck. We also need a system for us to be truly seen by our peers and co-workers. Without that our self-esteem plummets, our stress levels rise. Our fears drive us inward, in the direction of doubt and uncertainty. We know this as surely as we understand the intricate ways our physical, psychological and social selves interconnect. Every system within every organisation must support this. And this is the perfect moment to do so when there is nothing to lose and everything to gain.

Reinventions

My mission in this world, Bartleby, is to furnish you with office-room for such period as you may see fit to remain.

Herman Melville,
Bartleby, the Scrivener: A Story of Wall Street

The world wavered and quivered and threatened to burst into flames.

Virginia Woolf, *Mrs Dalloway*

Work as the professional class knew it stopped in early 2020 and the Nowhere Office officially came into existence. How long will this new phase last? We simply do not know. In the here and now (or perhaps, the *now-here*) one thing we do know: work never stopped, it just relocated, largely because of the internet.

There is a striking description at the beginning of Chris Kane's book *Where is My Office?* of Mark Thompson, former chief executive of the *New York Times*, going into the pandemic-empty offices in midtown Manhattan and cycling around the empty desks of the 'Old Grey Lady's' HQ.[1] Eighteen months later, in his exit interview, he said that: 'We're now a digital title in a digital world.'[2] All that happened to desk-based, meeting-based, knowledge-based work was the pandemic broke the last threads holding the embedded customs and practices together. This is how change happens: slowly and then all of a sudden completely. The world reinvents itself as if nothing ever happened.

As cultural commentator Seth Godin wrote in the summer of 2021:

> The last forty years have taught us that the technology that most disrupts established industries is speed. The speed of connection to peers, to suppliers and most of all, to customers. The speed of decision making, of ignoring sunk costs and of coordinated action. The internet has pushed all of these things forward, and we've just discovered, the office was holding all of them back.[3]

So we do need to reinvent professional work now that the one-size-fits-all model of the office is broken. Personally, I don't advocate or anticipate a wholesale revolution in the office to the degree that the fundamentals of capitalism get over-thrown, not only because I don't think it is going to happen but because I can't think of a sustainable economic alternative. But, that said, the pandemic shook the snow globe of working life more dramatically and decisively than many of us wanting deep structural change to office life and the management of work could ever have hoped for (even if the circumstances of such a catalyst were dreadful).

The back office, the front office, the office for newbies versus the office for those transitioning through the revolving doors of life: this is the true Nowhere Office and it is going to be different for everyone. Those who innovate to make productivity, purpose, culture and community the governing principles of the workplace and not the time, place or present-eeism of old will gain trust, authority, and people will flock to them. The future of work won't be one with no office – far from it – but it will be one with new identities and new systems thinking underpinning performance.

How far ahead can we look with any accuracy? Not far at all. Too much is shifting, and timeframes are collapsing (the Optimism Years and the Mezzanine Years both lasted around thirty years, but the Co-Working Years just thirteen). So let's look no further than the near nowhere of 2025. Just by way of context, that is when we will be either at or very near the point when the first AI machine is predicted to join a board of directors.[4] We will be well on the way to delivering mass tourist travel to space, and IBM's 1,000-qubit chip, IBM Quantum Condor, will already be complete. But despite all of this incredible technological advancement, I remain optimistic that shifting human-centred systems and human-centred policy and practice will impact on working life equal to anything the 3D internet era brings.

By the time the Nowhere Office began there was little of the optimistic spirit or sense of shared endeavour and purpose which the world of 1945 ushered in, and it is time to reclaim it as the post-pandemic world rebuilds and reimagines itself. I would therefore like to finish with a summary of twelve hybrid recommendation/predictions for those of us in the professions to take stock of and put in place as the new normal by 2025, so we can get better at office life and so that office life can itself get better.

1. *Healthy Hybrid*
A universal commitment to implement hybrid working intelligently and sustainably. It has to be functional and support social health and benefit everyone involved in the human supply chain of work – from innovator to implementer. If hybrid ends up alienating some workers, or penalising others, that's not workable. To create workplaces which have a healthy

hybrid mix of office and remote-based means iterating and trialling different models. These new ways of working will only succeed if employers are willing to listen to their employees who are, for the most part, emboldened by the realisation that their time and concentration is a valuable commodity and bargaining tool. The Leader as listener is crucial here. But workers need to regard hybrid as a way to get their best work done and not a disguised way to work less for the same money. Compromise and standardise: these will become the watchwords, along with a new recognition that nothing is for ever – you can change the hybrid model workplace by workplace, project by project, and to some extent, person by person. It's called flexibility and there is no reason why it cannot be healthy rather than heavy going. Global institutions from the World Bank, the International Labour Organisation and the World Economic Forum to innovative new organisations such as the World Experience Organization[5] should regularly benchmark healthy hybrid and monitor its successes and failures on a global level.

2. *Post-Presenteeism*
Technology doesn't need to sleep or stop, but humans do. We function best when we are able to adapt our sleep and waking hours to suit our own rhythms and needs.[6] The Nowhere Office will recognise and respect that fixed hours and schedules rely on choice, consent and customisation. Some people are horrified by the idea of splitting work duties across seven days, but for others this is liberating, creating air pockets of free time rather than a single 'weekend'. Post-presenteeism recognises that other priorities are emerging than old norms set down in different times for different generations. If you can bring your whole self to work, regardless of when and where you work, your productivity is likely to flourish. Knowledge

work should always be about being trusted to deliver for an organisation which offers splendid community, communication and culture (and, ideally, coffee). Trust is key to post-presenteeism. Task not time management should become top of the agenda. Nevertheless, agreed schedules will matter more, not less. Saying you will attend a meeting and then letting your colleagues down by saying 'Oh, I'll join by Zoom, something has come up', is not cool. Nor is being required to be 'always on' or under digital surveillance which monitors toilet breaks: that is presenteeism through the back door. Boundaries between digital and offline are essential. Email-free days, or periods of time for task-related work blocked out in diaries, should become the norm. What will matter is 'presence' not presenteeism – how you bring yourself to work and your attitude to it. If your team can be present even if they are physically not present, great. If not, ask why not, rather than demanding everyone comes back into the office 'just because'. Job applicants should know whether they are going to be working for a 'post-presenteeism' employer as a new kind of quality kitemark.

3. *Universities of Life and Social Clubs*
Corporate offices and HQs will have to recognise that in the future they are directly competing with coffee shops, clubs, co-working spaces, conference centres, and anywhere which appeals to people's sense of self and of creativity. The office as a physical space will therefore need to become a place for people to connect, learn and socialise in. It will have to reflect the fact that almost all actual digital work can be done elsewhere or remotely. The desk is all but over as a built-in feature of office life. Sofas, small theatres, spaces to convene and converse in will be 'in'. Corporate property developers and landlords, architects and designers will start to work more

closely with behavioural psychologists, anthropologists and sociologists to build around systems thinking, holistically. The siloed thinking in which an office space is rented or purchased without any thought to what happens inside it is, thankfully, over. In terms of design itself, modelling office spaces as a cross between an airline lounge and a private members' club is a good place to start: acknowledge that people are in transit, encourage movement, make them comfortable and relaxed while they are there. Repurpose office space and rediscover the power good buildings and design can bring to people's way of being with each other. Even if you do this, providing day passes for co-working spaces will also become the norm for organisations who recognise that the space between home and HQ, the stopping-off point, may well be a local co-working space. The Nowhere Office where work can nevertheless be productively done.

4. *VR Meets IRL*

The pandemic forced us to overcome any resistance to technology. If you haven't invested enough in technology to support your organisation, now is the time to do so. The next phase is virtual reality and the metaverse, whether we like it or not. As people spend less time in the same room together, the virtual room will become better than a buffering Zoom and a chorus of 'you're on mute'. We will feel more confident that we can work on the move and yet the culture to turn off and separate tech – not to be on your mobile phone in the company of others – will also become stronger. Being in-person will be seen as somewhat superior to being present with the prop of tech all the time. Meaningful disconnection – what the British trade union Prospect calls 'the right to disconnect' will become a much bigger discussion.[7] Cigarettes used to be in every hand and a highball was normal every day after work – but social mores change. So by 2025 it will become standard to leave technology at the door for certain occasions and the value of being in-person will be seen for the premium that it is. That said, all organisations need stronger back-up plans for when the technology stutters and stops or is interfered with by cybercrime. Fire and safety drills should be joined by cyberfail drills: this will be seen as essential office maintenance.

5. *Working Less, Working Better*

Hybrid working is going to usher in more part-time, flexible work. The strategies and policies around this will develop far more quickly than at any point over the last seventy years, will become much more widespread and will be separate from discussions about being in-person or remote. The ability to work less should be far more widely available with the caveat that certain jobs at certain times need full-time attention. But the idea that it's OK to work less and to be more productive has to become mainstream. We can make the blended lives we lead work better for us, become more productive and reduce the effect of stress and ill health on ourselves and on the economy if we learn to take advantage of placeless, timeless possibilities. But if we don't, the distinction between the hybrid have and the hybrid have-nots – whether you are a worker with agency over where and when you work or not – will lead to more inequality not less. Expect organisations to publish their policies on flexible working which go beyond the formal legal 'right to request' and to state a suite of options ranging from the four-day week to Arup's seven-day 'Work Unbound' to Fujitsu's 'Shift' model.[8]

6. *Pricing in Purpose*

I certainly agree with the economists Diane Coyle of the University of Cambridge and Leonard Nakamura of the Federal

Reserve Bank of Philadelphia Research Department who believe that 'a measure of welfare should become part of a system of accounts'.[9] In practice this means that root and branch reform of the way organisations run needs to continue so that inequalities are addressed and the workforce can trust that there is a point to their time and expertise. This will mean that instead of publishing outward-facing mission statements for the public, organisations will focus on giving clear signals to their people of how they intend to treat them and be far more accountable on this than before. We will see innovative organisations volunteering to publish their own 'Glassdoor' rankings of how they are rated by employees and subcontractors.[10]

7. *Bring Social Health into Well-being*

The Nowhere Office will be one in which well-being is seen in the broader context of social health. Organisations will start to promote healthy function across the whole organisation as well as promote individual physical and mental health. I anticipate that the World Health Organisation will finally get round to updating its definition of health to include twenty-first-century social health, not twentieth-century pre-digital social well-being. How the workplace communicates, is managed and learns, is all part of well-being. The coordination of networks is also crucial in a hybrid workplace. The chief people officer could soon be joined by the chief network officer to help connect people and improve their access to networks, enabling what and who they know to be shared in a more systematic and productive way internally. Finally, applying the model of the blended hybrid family to bring work colleagues together in a secular celebration of the work itself will become an important way to create corporate cohesion. 'Annual Report' could take on a celebratory, inclusive feel rather than a dry publishing exercise; celebrating well-being of the organisation as well as individual milestone moments such as worker birthdays should become the norm.

8. *Culture Wars Can Declare Peace*

It is thirty years since Henri Tajfel's 'in and out groups' of Social Identity Theory coincided with the era of identity politics.[11] By the time the Nowhere Office began the culture wars were in full flow. Will it matter as much in a world where you are a Learner, Leaver or Leader, working full time, part time, flexibly, remotely, hybrid, how you identify yourself in a private capacity as well? The transition to hybrid requires new equalising attitudes for new times. The old uniforms of work identity are dissolving into those which focus on tasks and time. Workplaces should be primarily about the work, where the individual identity of workers is respected and accepted as background, not foreground. We must bring our best selves to work in the Nowhere Office because there is nowhere to go without tolerance and respect.

9. *The Rise of the Solopreneur*

Because so many professionals will end up working freelance, or subcontracted, a new unifying identity is emerging for those responsible for making their own luck through their careers: the solopreneur. In an increasingly freelance working world, redesigning the fiscal basis of freelance work, tax breaks, homeworking allowances and the infrastructure for the freelance and portfolio 'portable professional' will matter as much as trying to attract and retain talent. Organisations will stop pretending that people are on a long-term career progression in one company and start to treat those who work for them as roving ambassadors for their brand who will better represent them if they have had good experiences working with them as part of an inevitably larger portfolio of projects or clients.

10. *Power Switch*

Managers and leaders have to completely reframe who works for them and who works *with* them, and operate in a completely new way. Remote-first businesses are making inroads against the old bricks-and-mortar businesses because they recognise that people want to work with others, but for their own satisfaction and not for a faceless entity. If you don't recognise this you are unlikely to make the cut as a brand or business that can attract talent or treat talent well. Talent is of course also part of your customer base, your client base, your consumer base. The balance of power is also adjusting as we understand more about the benefits of diverse thinking to avoid groupthink, be socially fairer and also foster innovation. This is the diversity dividend.

11. *Scale Back (and KISS)*

Small is better than big. Simple is better than complex. Remember the mantra 'Keep it Simple, Stupid', or KISS.[12] The Nowhere Office club and village envisaged by Charles Handy is local, collegiate, human and operates in keeping with the data showing that not only does innovation thrive better in smaller teams, but a simplified, decluttered way of working achieves better strategic results too. We need to review all management systems and operational procedures to be as direct and as straightforward as possible, and prioritise communication which conveys the essence of what success looks like – and drop the rest. In terms of investment in networks, remember too that small and simple is better. Trust itself is simple and intimate and thrives in smaller-scale situations. For this reason less money will go on putting on big conferences or sending people to them. Instead, the simplicity of allowing a wider pool of workers the time and expense to go for a long lunch (or a short coffee) to help them develop and build social capital, confidence and networks will be the single most effective innovation any organisation can implement.

12. *Re-Humanise Human Resources*
The metaverse, where headsets and virtual reality mediate all of our interactions is closer than we think and resistance may end up being futile.[13] We must, however, recognise that we humans are still the drivers of whatever specific technology we deploy and when, and that our work is still underpinned by distinctly human strengths: the ability to form relationships, instinct, feeling, passion, none of which is easily recreated digitally. Those in charge of human resources, the HR/People departments (the labels change but the meaning doesn't) are at the vanguard of this change. Many have their talents stuck by marzipan management layers that need to be released.

HR has become a cluttered cupboard, overlaid by complex systems and tech-led outsourcing. It is often in the front line to defend management rather than to look out for those reporting to them – an in-built conflict of interest which will no longer be acceptable. This almost certainly means that the Human Resource functions will become more clearly delineated and some tasks split: recruitment, onboarding, training and responsibility for social cohesion and networks can and should be separate from performance management, conflict resolution, firing, exit management. The skills for different tasks need to be reappraised. HR is not a one-size-fits-all department and it has become one. Ultimately if it declutters, re-establishes trust and limits automated management it will pay dividends. Put the human back in the corporate machine!

The Reinvention of Nowhere

Right now we are in a new mezzanine moment, a new co-working phase in which everything feels dominated by uncertainty and asymmetry. We must remain optimistic. The volatile snow globe of the Nowhere Office will settle (as snow globes always do in the end). But it would be a great shame not to get ahead of the curve and use the opportunity to remake workplace patterns *now/here* which better reflect who we are when we work, and how work is experienced. We may be nowhere but it turns out that this is in fact a good and also exciting place to be.

Acknowledgements

If I still had an office, I would have had to take more space to accommodate the people who helped me get this book written. Mistakes, errors and anything that doesn't work: that's on me. The good stuff: I owe to everyone else listed here.

It began with Polly Mackenzie at the British think-tank Demos who invited me to chair the Workshift Commission in December 2020 and write the paper which has led to this book. To Polly, a huge thank-you. My speaking agents Eithne Jones of Speaker Ideas and Leo von Bülow-Quirk of VBQ Speakers have kept me busy addressing audiences and developing my ideas throughout the long lockdowns. My book agent Elizabeth Sheinkman of PFD has been simply brilliant. I was delighted that through her I met my editors Sarah Caro at Basic Books UK and Clive Priddle at Public Affairs in America. Although this is my sixth book it is my first with them, and I learned a huge amount from such publishing aficionados. Their teams at Hachette, including Siam Hatzaw, Caroline Westmore, Anupama Roy-Chaudhury, Martin Bryant, have also been super helpful and great to work with. It has been lovely working again with the great Ruth Killick on UK publicity and Jocelynn Pedro and Lindsay Frankoff in America.

Sophie Radice and I have worked and socialised together now quite literally for over fifty years – and we still feel young! It was to Sophie I turned to help me complete the journalistic endeavour required for a topical book like this. She became my 'Book Mama' and I'm indebted to her. I'm also grateful to Calum McCrae, producer of The Nowhere Office podcast, who also helped with some of this book's back-office tasks, as did Roman Bamping who catalogued the citations and books.

My husband Alaric stress-tests every argument and is my constant sounding board. The family always grumble, rightly, when they see the book gleam in my eye because it means less of me around the dinner table but they always, always support me. 'It'll be fine, Mum' are always good words to hear.

I am incredibly lucky to have a broad network. Many here took the time and trouble to be interviewed and to send their experiences. Others have guided me with useful articles and opinions, or have been sounding boards. These people are all as perspicacious as they are generous. Melis Abacıoğlu; Tom Adeyoola, Esther Akpovi; Jeremy Apfel; Mary Appleton; Mohit Bakaya; Matt Ballantine; Stephen Barber; Pierpaulo Barbieri; Cathryn Barnard; Jonny Bealby; Mark Bergman; Margaret Bluman; Harshna Brahbhatt; Helen Brocklebank; Sir Vince Cable; Rohan Candappa; Louise Chester; Sir Cary Cooper; Caroline Corby; Hilary Cottam; Henry Coutinho-Mason; Fin Craig; Michael Creamer; Bruce Daisley; Matthew d'Ancona; Gaby Darbyshire; Andrew Davidson; Tim Davie; Dana Denis-Smith; Elizabeth Diaferia; Pamela Dow; Rose Eccleshare; William Eccleshare; Dave Eisenberg; Kevin Ellis; Mark Eltringham; Niall Ferguson; Eliza Filby; Carl Benedikt Frey; Alan Gemmell; Giles Gibbons; Emma Gilpin-Jacobs; Anna Graham; Lynda Gratton; Josh Greene; Charles Handy; Eric Hazan; Ayesha Hazarika; Anoushka Healy; Bruce Hellman; John Hendy QC; Graham Hitchen; Andy Hobsbawm; Lucy Hooberman; Herminia Ibarra; Emma Jacobs; Elsbeth Johnson;

Chris Kane; David Katz; Elizabeth Katz; Barbara Kellerman; Helena Kennedy; Rose Lasko-Skinner; Kirsten Lass; Fiona Legg; Charles Lewington; Gemma Lines; Joy Lo Dico; Hamish McRae; Yasmina Memarian; Liz Moseley; Elliot Moss; Anne-Elisabeth Moutet; Bejay Mulenga; Niall Murphy; Tanya Murphy; Sanjay Nazerali; Jacqueline Nettl; Dan Newman; Susie Orbach; Dennis Owusu-Sem; Ben Page; Andrew Pakes; Rimma Perelmuter; Judy Piatkus; Ed Pilkington; Sarah Pinch; Linda Plant; Jake Pugh; Henry Richards; Jo Scard; Anya Schiffrin; Alice Sherwood; David Shriver; Saskia Sissons; Sir Martin Sorrell; Andrew St George; Wendell Steavenson; Stefan Stern; Jack Stoerger; Joanna Swash; Chris Thurling; Deborah Unger; Michael Vachon; James Wallman; Rachael Ward; Lewis Wedlock; Sarah Willett; Adrian Wooldridge.

During the writing of this book I had some physical health problems and would like to thank the following for their tremendous expertise and kindness. Harry Petrushkin and his team at Moorfields Eye Hospital, and Alison Savory and Gloria Else: their hybrid health solutions of Eastern acupuncture and Traditional Chinese Medicine combined beautifully with the Western treatments. And to the peerless Ed Blake of Physio Ed. Many, many thanks, all.

I am also grateful to three people who I can no longer phone or zoom or see in person, and what a terrible wrench that is. I had begun to have regular conversations about the topics covered in this book with Derek Draper, the entrepreneurial psychologist and leadership writer before Covid-19 changed his life for ever. I remain hopeful he can recover and we can resume these conversations. My great friend and inspiration Jessica Morris finally lost her battle to beat glioblastoma just as I completed the first draft. Finally, I owe a constant debt to my late father, Eric Hobsbawm. He gave me the gift of curiosity and confidence. His vintage mint green

Hermes Ambassador typewriter stands on a shelf above my reading chair at home and I take it as silent encouragement: '*Nur weil die dinge so sind, wie sie sind, heißt das nicht, dass sie so bleiben.*'

Notes

Preface

1. @Tobi, 21 May 2020, 3:55 p.m., Twitter, https://twitter.com/tobi/status/1263483496087064579?ref_src=twsrc%5Etfw
2. Data shows that 41 per cent of the US workforce, 64 million people, as of 2018 were classed as professionals: https://www.dpeaflcio.org/factsheets/the-professional-and-technical-workforce-by-the-numbers
3. Studs Terkel, *Working: People Talk About What They Do All Day and How They Feel About What They Do* (New Press, 1974)
4. World Health Organisation, 'Mental Health and Substance Use: Mental Health in the Workplace', https://www.who.int/teams/mental-health-and-substance-use/promotion-prevention/mental-health-in-the-workplace; see also 'What a Work-From-Home Revolution Means for Commercial Property', *The Economist*, 5 June 2021, https://www.economist.com/finance-and-economics/2021/06/03/what-a-work-from-home-revolution-means-for-commercial-property
5. See 'The Great Resignation: Why People Are Leaving Their Jobs in Growing Numbers', NPR, 22 October 2021, https://www.npr.org/2021/10/22/1048332481/the-great-resignation-why-people-are-leaving-their-jobs-in-growing-numbers; US Bureau of Labor Statistics, 'Job Openings and Labor Turnover Summary', 12 October 2021, https://www.bls.gov/news.release/jolts.nro.htm?utm_source=npr_newsletter&utm_medium=email&utm_content=20211018&utm_term=5879628&utm_

campaign=money&utm_id=4858467&orgid=&utm_att1=money

6. 'Increasingly, Workers Expect Pandemic Workplace Adaptations to Stick', *Prudential Pulse of America Survey*, 6 April 2021, https://news.prudential.com/increasingly-workers-expect-pandemic-workplace-adaptations-to-stick.htm; Ashley Stahl, 'The Future of Offices and Workspaces, Post-Pandemic', *Forbes*, 16 April 2021, https://www.forbes.com/sites/ashleystahl/2021/04/16/the-future-of-offices-and-workspaces-post-pandemic/?sh=388df2006442; see also Matthew DiLallo, 'Commercial Real Estate Investing Statistics 2021', Millionacres, 16 November 2020, https://www.millionacres.com/research/commercial-real-estate-investing-statistics/; and for specific prediction of 80 per cent occupancy see Erik Sherman, 'Delta Disrupts Office Return Plans: What Now?', GlobeSt.com, 13 September 2021, https://www.globest.com/2021/09/13/delta-disrupts-office-return-plans-what-now/?slreturn=20210901045552

7. McKinsey Global Institute, 'The Future of Work After Covid-19', 18 February 2021, https://www.mckinsey.com/featured-insights/future-of-work/the-future-of-work-after-covid-19

8. 'Management, professional and related occupations' according to the US bureau of Labor Statistics, May 2020, https://www.bls.gov/oes/current/oes_stru.htm

Introduction

1. International Labour Organization, *World Employment and Social Outlook Trends 2020*, International Labour Office, Geneva, https://www.ilo.org/wcmsp5/groups/public/---dgreports/---dcomm/---publ/documents/publication/wcms_734455.pdf

2. 'Number of Employees Worldwide in 2020, by Region and Sector (in Millions)', Statista, 2021, https://www.statista.com/statistics/962868/global-employment-region-sector/

3. 'The Professional and Technical Workforce: By the Numbers',

2021 Fact Sheet, Department for Professional Employees, 27 September 2021, https://www.dpeaflcio.org/factsheets/the-professional-and-technical-workforce-by-the-numbers

4. 'The Future of Jobs Report 2020', World Economic Forum, 20 October 2020, https://www.weforum.org/reports/the-future-of-jobs-report-2020; see also McKinsey Global Institute, 'The Future of Work After Covid-19', 18 February 2021, https://www.mckinsey.com/featured-insights/future-of-work/the-future-of-work-after-covid-19; 'More Than Half of Employees Globally Would Quit Their jobs if Not Provided Post-Pandemic Flexibility', 21 May 2021, https://www.ey.com/en_ro/news/2021/05/ey-study--more-than-half-of-employees-globally-would-quit-their-; Department for Professional Employees, AFL-CIO, 'The Professional and Technical Workforce: By the Numbers', 2021 Fact Sheet, 27 September 2021, https://www.dpeaflcio.org/factsheets/the-professional-and-technical-workforce-by-the-numbers

5. See data from Office for National Statistics Coronavirus (Covid-19) Latest Insights: Work, https://www.ons.gov.uk/peoplepopulationandcommunity/healthandsocialcare/conditionsanddiseases/articles/coronaviruscovid19latestinsights/work; and the World Bank: Michael Weber and David Newhouse, 'These Types of Workers Were Most Impacted by the Covid-19 Pandemic', World Bank Blogs, 23 September 2021, https://blogs.worldbank.org/jobs/these-types-workers-were-most-impacted-covid-19-pandemic

6. See Leesman, 'Workplace 2021: Appraising Future-Readiness', https://www.leesmanindex.com/media/Leesman-Workplace-2021-Report-1.pdf; and McKinsey, 'Future of Work', https://www.mckinsey.com/featured-insights/future-of-work

7. Peter Scott and Guy Judge, 'Cycles and Steps in British Commercial Property Values', *Applied Economics*, 32 (10): 1287–97, https://www.researchgate.net/publication/24074467_Cycles_and_Steps_in_British_Commercial_Property_Values

8. 'Global Commercial Real Estate: Market Size 2005–2007',

IbisWorld, 2 August 2021, https://www.ibisworld.com/global/market-size/global-commercial-real-estate/

9. Carl Sandburg, 'Skyscraper', *Chicago Poems* (University of Illinois Press, 1992)

10. See Martin Wolf, *The Shifts and the Shocks: What We've Learned – and Have Still to Learn – from the Financial Crisis* (Allen Lane, 2014)

11. Nicholson Baker, *The Mezzanine* (Granta, 2011)

12. The metaverse of virtual reality became thrown into the public spotlight at the end of 2021 when Facebook's parent company name was rebranded by Mark Zuckerberg as 'Meta'. The original phrase was coined in Neal Stephenson's 1992 novel, *The Snow Crash*; Daniel Villareal, 'What is "Snow Crash"? Twitter Compares Facebook's "Metaverse" Announcement to '90s Novel', *Newsweek*, 28 October 2021, https://www.newsweek.com/what-snow-crash-twitter-compares-facebooks-metaverse-announcement-90s-dystopian-sci-fi-1643690

13. Amy Greenshields, 'Covid-19 Forces One of the Biggest Surges in Tech Investment in History, Finds World's Largest Tech Leadership', KPMG, 22 September 2020, https://home.kpmg/xx/en/home/media/press-releases/2020/09/covid-19-forces-one-of-the-biggest-surges-in-technology-investment-in-history-finds-worlds-largest-technology-leadership-survey.html; McKinsey, 'Global Business-Services Sourcing Comes of Age', 1 September 2021, https://www.mckinsey.com/business-functions/operations/our-insights/global-business-services-sourcing-comes-of-age

14. See 'The New Future of Work Project', Microsoft, https://www.microsoft.com/en-us/research/project/the-new-future-of-work/

Chapter 1: Shift 1: Placeless, Timeless

1. Urban Omnibus and Rosalie Genevro, 'A Walk with Frank Duffy', Urban Omnibus, Architectural League of New York,

8 July 2009, https://urbanomnibus.net/2009/07/a-walk-with-frank-duffy/

2. See Tim Oldman, *Why Workplace: A Leader's Guide to Rebuilding the Post-Pandemic Workplace*, Leesman, October 2021, https://www.leesmanindex.com/media/Leesman-Why-Workplace-Guide-DPS-final.pdf?eid=CiLoqOwTVIfQWziIWqM6INZlBg6D8JOL%2BNZOb88wOzoxGQ%2FPSsFldoOrC8FwbwFelpHsyMm48GqbPS8Yy%2B8wam7Y7uMPTQOt18Hgv52BoygfnYK4

3. 'Number of Freelancers in the United States from 2017 to 2028 (in Millions)', September 2017, Statista, https://www.statista.com/statistics/921593/gig-economy-number-of-freelancers-us/; PwC US Remote Work Survey, 12 January 2021, https://www.pwc.com/us/en/library/covid-19/us-remote-work-survey.html

4. 'Number of Smartphones Sold to End Users Worldwide from 2007 to 2021 (in Million Units)', Statista, February 2021, https://www.statista.com/statistics/263437/global-smartphone-sales-to-end-users-since-2007/

5. 2021 Work Trend Index: Annual Report, *The Next Great Disruption is Hybrid Work – Are We Ready?*, 22 March 2021, https://ms-worklab.azureedge.net/files/reports/hybridWork/pdf/2021_Microsoft_WTI_Report_March.pdf

6. See also Ria Patel, 'Arup's New Hybrid Work Model Allows 6,000 UK Employees to Choose Their Working Days Across a Seven-Day Week in New Era for Flexibly Working', Arup, 20 May 2021, https://www.arup.com/news-and-events/arups-new-hybrid-work-model-allows-6000-uk-employees-to-choose-their-working-days

7. Sara Bean, 'Digital Mobility to Work Anytime, Anywhere is Key to Job Satisfaction', Workplace Insight, 26 May 2016, https://workplaceinsight.net/ability-work-anytime-anywhere-now-key-job-satisfaction/

8. Mark Bergen, 'Google Wants People in Office, Despite Productivity Gains at Home', Bloomberg, 15 July 2021, https://www.bloomberg.com/news/articles/2021-07-15/google-

googl-wants-employees-to-return-to-office-despite-productivity-gains

9. 'Young People and Working from Home (WFH) in the Pandemic', Ipsos MORI, 9 March 2021, https://www.ipsos.com/ipsos-mori/en-uk/young-people-and-working-home-wfh-pandemic

10. 'Looking After Children and Working from Home (WFH) in the Pandemic', Ipsos MORI, 16 March 2021, https://www.ipsos.com/ipsos-mori/en-uk/looking-after-children-and-working-home-wfh-pandemic

11. 'Vodafone Global Survey Reveals Rapid Adoption of Flexible Working', Vodafone, 8 February 2016, https://newscentre.vodafone.co.uk/press-release/974/; see also Eir Nolsoe, 'One in Four Businesses Intend to Allow All Workers to Work from Home at Least Some of the Time', YouGov, 29 July 2021, https://yougov.co.uk/topics/economy/articles-reports/2021/07/29/one-four-businesses-intend-allow-all-workers-work-

12. Alison Velati, 'Morgan Stanley Chief Talks Tough on Return to the Office', *Financial Times*, 14 June 2021, https://www.ft.com/content/ffd6033f-e8fc-4289-85b2-42bc4ddddd16

13. 'Goldman Sachs, Bank Boss Rejects Work from Home as the "New Normal"', *BBC News*, 25 February 2021, https://www.bbc.co.uk/news/business-56192048

14. William Cohan, 'My Years on Wall Street Showed Me Why You Can't Make a Deal on Zoom', *New York Times*, 16 August 2021, https://www.nytimes.com/2021/08/16/opinion/covid-wall-street-delta-office.html

15. Vicky McKeever, 'UK Accountancy Giant Tells Its 22,000 Staff They Can Start and Finish Their Working Day When They Like', CNBC Make It, 31 March 2021, https://www.cnbc.com/2021/03/31/pwc-tells-uk-staff-they-can-start-and-finish-work-when-they-like.html

16. See ADP Research Institute, 'One Year Into the Pandemic: ADP Research Institute Uncovers How Working Conditions and Attitudes Have Changed in Global Study', ADP, 28 April

2021, https://mediacenter.adp.com/2021-04-28-One-Year-into-the-Pandemic-ADP-Research-Institute-R-Uncovers-How-Working-Conditions-and-Attitudes-Have-Changed-in-Global-Study?_ga=2.157230520.208485360.1635166473-1830634459.1635166473&_gl=1*1g8pgoi*_ga*MTgzMDYzNDQ1OS4xNjM1MTY2NDcz*_ga_Z7FCJ8MYEN*MTYzNTE2NjQ3Mi4xLjEuMTYzNTE2NjQ4Ni40oNg

17. See Tim Oldman, *Why Workplace: A Leader's Guide to Rebuilding the Post-Pandemic Workplace*, Leesman, October 2021, https://www.leesmanindex.com/media/Leesman-Why-Workplace-Guide-DPS-final.pdf?eid=CiLoqOwTVIfQWziIWqM6INZlBg6D8JOL%2BNZOb88wOzoxGQ%2FPSsFldoOrC8FwbwFelpHsyMm48GqbPS8Yy%2B8wam7Y7uMPTQOt18Hgv52BoygfnYK4

18. Freddie Steele, 'WeWork partners With Cushman & Wakefield on Flexible Working Offer', Workplace Insight, 10 August 2021, https://workplaceinsight.net/wework-partners-with-cushman-wakefield-on-flexible-working-offer/

19. '5 Reasons Real Estate Could Roar in the 2020s', *Institutional Investor*, 11 August 2021, https://www.institutionalinvestor.com/article/b1sq9nsshqkpw6/5-Reasons-Real-Estate-Could-Roar-in-the-2020s; David M. Levitt, 'Office Building Terraces Bloom During Covid', Commercial Observer, 31 August 2021, https://commercialobserver.com/2021/08/office-building-terraces-cost-maintenance/

20. See also the emergence of the World Experience Organization during the pandemic, https://www.worldxo.org/

21. 'Google May Cut Pay of Staff Who Work from Home', *BBC News*, 11 August 2021, https://www.bbc.co.uk/news/business-58171716

22. Sarah O'Connor, 'Cutting Pay for Remote Workers is a Risky Move', *Financial Times*, 17 August 2021, https://www.ft.com/content/a37150e3-7480-4181-90e4-1ce9dc5d1d39

23. Zoe Schiffer, 'Apple Employees Push Back Against Returning to the Office in Internal Letter', *Verge*, 4 June 2021, https://

www.theverge.com/2021/6/4/22491629/apple-employees-push-back-return-office-internal-letter-tim-cook

24. '11.8% CAGR, Employee Communication Software Market is Emerging with $1,780.09 Million by 2027', *Industry Today*, 8 June 2021, https://industrytoday.co.uk/it/11-8--cagr--employee-communication-software-market-is-emerging-with--1-780-09-million-by-2027

25. See https://grooveapp.io/community

26. McKinsey Global Institute, 'What's Next for Remote Work: An Analysis of 2,000 Tasks, 800 Jobs, and Nine Countries', McKinsey, 23 November 2020, https://www.mckinsey.com/featured-insights/future-of-work/whats-next-for-remote-work-an-analysis-of-2000-tasks-800-jobs-and-nine-countries

27. 'Quality of Life at Home, Exploring People's Perceptions of Where They Live Before and During Lockdown', Quality of Life Foundation, August 2020, https://www.qolf.org/wp-content/uploads/2020/08/QOL_QualityOfLifeAtHome_August2020_5MB.pdf

28. 'What a Work-from-Home Revolution Means for Commercial Property', *The Economist*, 5 June 2021, https://www.economist.com/finance-and-economics/2021/06/03/what-a-work-from-home-revolution-means-for-commercial-property

29. Doreen Massey, 'A Global Sense of Place', *Marxism Today*, June 1991, http://banmarchive.org.uk/collections/mt/pdf/91_06_24.pdf

30. @HerminiaIbarra, 7 September 2021, 7:44 a.m., Twitter, https://twitter.com/HerminiaIbarra/status/1435131793401843714; see more of her work at www.herminiaibarra.com

31. Blake Thorne, 'How Distractions at Work Take Up More Time Than You Think', I Done This Blog, 13 February 2020, http://blog.idonethis.com/distractions-at-work/

32. Adam Gorlick, 'The Productivity Pitfalls of Working from Home in the Age of Covid-19', Stanford News, 30 March 2020, https://news.stanford.edu/2020/03/30/productivity-pitfalls-working-home-age-covid-19/; see also Jose Maria Barrero, Nicholas Bloom, and Steven J. Davis, 'Why Working

from Home Will Stick', National Bureau of Economic Research, April 2021, https://www.nber.org/papers/w28731; also Nicholas Bloom et al., 'Does Working from Home Work? Evidence from a Chinese Experiment', National Bureau of Economic Research, March 2013, https://www.nber.org/papers/w18871

33. Hochschild, Arlie Russell, *The Time Bind: When Work Becomes Home and Home Becomes Work* (Holt Paperbacks, 2001 [1997]); see also this interview with Hochschild: Julie Beck, 'The Concept Creep of "Emotional Labour"', *Atlantic*, 26 November 2018, https://www.theatlantic.com/family/archive/2018/11/arlie-hochschild-housework-isnt-emotional-labor/576637/

34. Alice Hancock and Philip Georgiadis, 'We Don't Know How Many People Will Choose to Fly', *Financial Times*, 14 January 2021, https://www.ft.com/content/867a5342-c94c-43f6-9783-a817443c9471; and Natasha Frost, 'Will Business Travel Ever be the Same?', BBC Worklife, 5 August 2020, https://www.bbc.com/worklife/article/20200731-how-coronavirus-will-change-business-travel

35. James Warrington, 'Transport for London Secures £1.08bn Emergency Funding Deal', *CITY AM*, 1 June 2021, https://www.cityam.com/transport-for-london-secures-1-08bn-emergency-funding-deal/; Glenday, John, 'TfL Left to Mind a Widening Ad Revenue Gap as Income Slumps £100m', The Drum, 6 July 2021, https://www.thedrum.com/news/2021/07/06/tfl-left-mind-widening-ad-revenue-gap-income-slumps-100m

36. 'Number of Freelancers in the United States from 2017 to 2028 (in Millions)', Statista, September 2017, https://www.statista.com/statistics/921593/gig-economy-number-of-freelancers-us/

37. Karen Gilchrist, 'The 10 Countries with the Fastest-Growing Earnings for Freelancers', CNBC, 6 August 2019, https://www.cnbc.com/2019/08/07/the-10-countries-with-the-fastest-growing-earnings-for-freelancers.html

38. Hannah Watkins, 'The Problem Isn't the Office – It's the Commute', Hubble, 17 August 2021, https://hubblehq.com/blog/impact-of-commute-time-on-work-preferences

39. Jerry Useem, 'The Psychological Benefits of Commuting to Work', *Atlantic*, 29 July 2021, https://www.theatlantic.com/magazine/archive/2021/07/admit-it-you-miss-your-commute/619007/

40. 'How Covid-19 Triggered the Digital and e-Commerce Turning Point', United Nations Conference on Trade and Development, 15 March 2021, https://unctad.org/news/how-covid-19-triggered-digital-and-e-commerce-turning-point

41. 'Southern California Renters are Moving to the Suburbs Post-Pandemic, Says New Study', Propertyfundsworld, 20 May 2021, https://www.propertyfundsworld.com/2021/05/20/300587/southern-california-renters-are-moving-suburbs-post-pandemic-says-new-study

42. David Sharman, 'Publisher Reveals it Now Employs More Journalists than in 2019', HoldtheFrontPage, 26 July 2021, https://www.holdthefrontpage.co.uk/2021/news/publisher-creates-more-new-roles-in-bid-to-return-staffing-to-pre-pandemic-levels/

43. Emma Simpson, 'Almost 50 Shops a Day Disappear from High Streets', BBC News, 5 September 2021, https://www.bbc.co.uk/news/business-58433461

44. See https://www.sohohouse.com/studio-spaces

45. Konrad Putzier, 'Saks Fifth Avenue Owner, WeWork to Run Co-Working Spaces in Former Stores', *Wall Street Journal*, 10 August 2021, https://www.wsj.com/articles/wework-to-run-co-working-spaces-in-some-saks-fifth-avenue-stores-11628596800

46. In October 2021 London Mayor Sadiq Khan introduced a punitive daily Ultra Low Emission Zone (ULEZ) tax on certain vehicles, https://tfl.gov.uk/modes/driving/ultra-low-emission-zone

47. 'Working From Home "Saves London Commuters 24 Days Per Year in Travel Time"', Netimperative, 8 July 2020, https://www.netimperative.com/2020/07/08/working-from-home-saves-london-commuters-24-days-per-year-in-travel-time/

48. 'Productivity Management Software Market Size, Share &

Trends Analysis Report by Deployment (On-Premise, Cloud), by Enterprise (Large Enterprise, SME), by Solution, by Region, and Segment Forecasts, 2021–2028', Grand View Research, July 2021, https://www.grandviewresearch.com/industry-analysis/productivity-management-software-market

49. Bertrand Russell, 'In Praise of Idleness', *In Praise of Idleness and Other Stories* (Routledge, 2004 [1935])

50. Charlie Giattino and Esteban Ortiz-Ospina, 'Are We Working More Than Ever?', 16 December 2020, Our World in Data, https://ourworldindata.org/working-more-than-ever

51. Michael Gibbs, Friederike Mengel, and Christoph Siemroth, 'Work from Home & Productivity: Evidence from Personnel & Analytics Data on IT Professionals', Becker Friedman Institute, 13 July 2021, https://bfi.uchicago.edu/working-paper/2021-56/

52. Naohiro Yashiro, 'Japan's Optional Four-Day Week Divides Workers', East Asia Forum, 21 August 2021, https://www.eastasiaforum.org/2021/08/21/japans-optional-four-day-week-divides-workers/

53. See the Gov.UK outlines of flexible working, https://www.gov.uk/flexible-working; see also 'Staff to Gain Right to Request Flexible Working from First Day', BBC News, 21 September 2021, https://www.bbc.co.uk/news/business-58636439

54. Nina Janza, 'Flexible Working Arrangements are on the Rise. Here's Why', Spica, 23 June 2021, https://www.spica.com/blog/flexible-working-arrangements-rising

55. See https://www.weforum.org/communities/gfc-on-the-new-agenda-for-work-wages-and-job-creation

56. Lynda Gratton, 'Any Time, Anywhere: What Does Hybrid Mean for Your Business?', London Business School, 2 June 2021, https://www.london.edu/think/any-time-anywhere-what-does-hybrid-mean-for-your-business; hear Lynda Gratton on the podcast The Nowhere Office in which these remarks were made in 2021, https://www.listennotes.com/podcasts/the-nowhere-office/introducing-the-nowhere-office-uUpLRy-m54e/;

see also Lynda Gratton and Andrew Scott, *The 100-Year Life: Living and Working in an Age of Longevity* (Bloomsbury, 2020)

57. 'Arup Embraces Seven-Day Work Week with Flexible Hours', Consultancy.uk, 21 May 2021, https://www.consultancy.uk/news/27991/arup-embraces-seven-day-work-week-with-flexible-hours

58. See 'Fujitsu Embarks Towards "New Normal", Redefining Working Styles for Its Japan Offices', 6 July 2020, https://www.fujitsu.com/global/about/resources/news/press-releases/2020/0706-01.html

59. Danielle Demetriou, 'How the Japanese are Putting an End to Extreme Work Weeks', BBC Worklife, 17 January 2020, https://www.bbc.com/worklife/article/20200114-how-the-japanese-are-putting-an-end-to-death-from-overwork

Chapter 2: Shift 2: Worker Beings

1. Catherine Salfino, 'Why Growth in Athleisure is the Pandemic's Silver Lining', Sourcing Journal, 13 August 2020, https://sourcingjournal.com/topics/lifestyle-monitor/coronavirus-athleisure-bcg-klaviyo-american-eagle-offline-aerie-npd-226232/

2. Tom Bottomley, 'Athleisure Orders Rise by 84% Since Start of Pandemic', The Industry.Fashion, 17 February 2021, https://www.theindustry.fashion/athleisure-orders-rise-by-84-since-start-of-pandemic/

3. Eric Rosenbaum, 'The Latest Numbers of How Many Workers Will be Returning to Offices, and How Often', CNBC, 8 July 2021, https://www.cnbc.com/2021/07/08/how-many-workers-will-be-returning-to-offices-and-how-often.html

4. Eamon Akil Farhat, 'London Staff Want Pay Rises to Return to Office, Survey Says', Bloomberg, 20 July 2021, https://www.bloomberg.com/news/articles/2021-07-20/london-staff-want-big-pay-rises-to-return-to-office-survey-says; Jack Kelly, 'California Congressman Mark Takano Introduces Legislation

for a Four-Day Workweek', *Forbes*, 29 July 2021, https://www.
forbes.com/sites/jackkelly/2021/07/29/california-congress-
man-mark-takano-introduced-legislation-for-a-four-day-work-
week/?sh=2637e0d8279d

5. Karen Kahn, 'Three Quarters of Americans Prefer to Work
for an Employee-Owned Company', Fifty by Fifty, 3 June
2019, https://www.fiftybyfifty.org/2019/06/three-quarters-of-
americans-prefer-to-work-for-an-employee-owned-company/

6. Richard Henderson and Patrick Temple-West, 'Group of US
Corporate Leaders Ditches Shareholder-First Mantra',
Financial Times, 19 August 2019, https://www.ft.com/content/
e21a9fac-c1f5-11e9-a8e9-296ca66511c9

7. 'One in Twenty Workers are in "Useless" Jobs – Far Fewer
Than Previously Thought', University of Birmingham, 3 June
2021, https://www.birmingham.ac.uk/news/latest/2021/06/
one-in-twenty-workers-are-in-'useless'-jobs---far-fewer-than-
previously-thought.aspx

8. 'The Next Normal Arrives: Trends That Will Define 2021 –
and Beyond', McKinsey, 4 January 2021, https://www.mckinsey.
com/featured-insights/leadership/the-next-normal-arrives-
trends-that-will-define-2021-and-beyondff

9. See annual LinkedIn Survey, '2021 Workplace Learning
Report', https://learning.linkedin.com/resources/workplace-
learning-report

10. See the British case of barrister Alison Bailey: Neil Rose,
'Chambers and Stonewall Fail to Strike Out Barrister's
Discrimination Claim', Legal Futures, 12 March 2021,
https://www.legalfutures.co.uk/latest-news/chambers-and-
stonewall-fail-to-strike-out-barristers-discrimination-claim

11. See 'The Boardroom Still Has a Gender Gap: Here's What it
Looks Like – and How to Fix It', World Economic Forum,
March 2021, https://www.weforum.org/agenda/2021/03/study-
shows-the-state-of-female-representation-on-corporate-boards

12. Interviewed for The Nowhere Office podcast, https://open.
spotify.com/show/3SAjjNiMYSNWQTMHazqcRS

13. 'The Future of Jobs Report 2020', World Economic Forum, October 2020, https://www.weforum.org/reports/the-future-of-jobs-report-2020/digest

14. For more data on generations see Pew Research Center, 'On the Cusp of Adulthood and Facing an Uncertain Future: What We Know About Gen Z So Far', https://www.pewresearch.org/social-trends/2020/05/14/on-the-cusp-of-adulthood-and-facing-an-uncertain-future-what-we-know-about-gen-z-so-far-2/; see also Bobby Duffy, *Generations: Does When You're Born Shape Who You Are?* (Atlantic, 2021)

15. For Rose Eccleshare's full interview, see Julia Hobsbawm, *The Nowhere Office*, Demos, March 2021, https://demos.co.uk/wp-content/uploads/2021/03/The-Nowhere-Office.pdf

16. Interviewed for The Nowhere Office podcast, https://open.spotify.com/show/3SAjjNiM

17. Ibid.

18. Brie Weiler Reynolds, 'Freelance Survey Results, Plus 30 Companies Hiring Freelancers', FlexJobs, https://www.flexjobs.com/blog/post/freelance-survey-results-plus-companies-hiring-freelancers/; see also Michael B. Arthur, 'Freelancing is for Baby Boomers Too – and There's More Than One Way to go About It', *Forbes*, 24 March 2019, https://www.forbes.com/sites/michaelbarthur/2019/03/24/freelancing-is-for-baby-boomers-too-and-theres-more-than-one-way-to-go-about-it/?sh=b8fd68c1b4c8

19. Josh Bersin, 'The Business Impact of HR Capabilities: It's Far Bigger Than You Thought', Joshbersin.com, 7 June 2021, https://joshbersin.com/2021/06/the-business-impact-of-hr-capabilities-its-far-bigger-than-you-thought/

20. George Dickson, 'Shopify's Brittany Forsyth on Scaling Company Culture', Bonusly, 13 April 2015 (updated 11 July 2019), blog https://blog.bonus.ly/shopifys-brittany-forsyth-on-scaling-culture/

Chapter 3: Shift 3: The Productivity Puzzle

1. Steve Newman, 'Martha Gellhorn – The Hospital Ship: June 6th–7th, 1944', 13 November 2018, https://stevenewmanwriter. medium.com/martha-gellhorn-the-hospital-ship-part-1-d7e8c54000e1

2. Allied Forces, 21st Army Group, *The Administrative History of the Operations of 21 Army Group on the Continent of Europe 6 June 1944–8 May 1945* (HQ BAOR, 1945)

3. Christian Krekel et al., 'Employee Wellbeing, Productivity, and Firm Performance: Evidence from 1.8 Million Employees', VOXeu, 21 April 2019, https://voxeu.org/article/employee-wellbeing-productivity-and-firm-performance

4. Michael Gibbs, Friederike Mengel, and Christoph Siemroth, 'Work from Home & Productivity: Evidence from Personnel & Analytics Data on IT Professionals', Becker Friedman Institute, 13 July 2021, https://bfi.uchicago.edu/working-paper/2021-56/

5. See Microsoft Work Trend Index 2021, https://www.microsoft.com/en-us/worklab/work-trend-index/hybrid-work; and the report itself, *The Next Great Disruption is Hybrid Work – Are We Ready*, 22 March 2021, https://ms-worklab.azureedge.net/files/reports/hybridWork/pdf/2021_Microsoft_WTI_Report_March.pdf

6. Jose Maria Barrero, Nicholas Bloom, and Steven J. Davis, 'Why Working from Home Will Stick', National Bureau of Economic Research, April 2021, https://www.nber.org/papers/w28731

7. George Halkos, and Dimitrios Bousinakis, 'The Effect of Stress and Satisfaction on Productivity', *International Journal of Productivity and Performance Management*, 22 June 2010, https://www.emerald.com/insight/content/doi/10.1108/17410401011052869/full/html

8. 'More on "Lying Flat"', Modern Chinese Literature and Culture Resource Center, 3 July 2021, https://u.osu.edu/mclc/2021/07/03/more-on-lying-flat/

9. Josh Cohen, *Not Working: Why We Have to Stop* (Granta, 2018)

10. Clay Skipper, 'Our Collective Fixation on Productivity is Older Than You Think', *GQ*, 1 February 2021, https://www.gq.com/story/james-suzman-work-interview

11. David Gelles, and David Yaffe-Bellany, 'Shareholder Value is No Longer Everything, Top C.E.O.s say', *New York Times*, 19 August 2019, https://www.nytimes.com/2019/08/19/business/business-roundtable-ceos-corporations.html

12. British Academy, 'Future of the Corporation', https://www.thebritishacademy.ac.uk/programmes/future-of-the-corporation/

13. https://corporate.walmart.com/global-responsibility

14. Barry Levine, 'Study: Gen Z Cares About Issues and is Skeptical of Brands', Marketing Dive, 30 May 2019, https://www.marketingdive.com/news/study-gen-z-cares-about-issues-and-is-skeptical-of-brands/555782/

15. https://www.businessofpurpose.com/statistics New Paradigm Strategy Group & Fortune, 2019

16. https://www.businessofpurpose.com/statistics DDI World, 2018

17. Zoe Schiffer, 'Apple Employees Push Back Against Returning to the Office in Internal Letter', *Verge*, 4 June 2021, https://www.theverge.com/2021/6/4/22491629/apple-employees-push-back-return-office-internal-letter-tim-cook

18. 'Machines Will Do More Tasks Than Humans by 2025: WEF', Phys.org, 17 September 2018, https://phys.org/news/2018-09-machines-tasks-humans-wef.html

19. Scott Stein, 'Virtual Mark Zuckerberg Showed Me Facebook's New VR Workplace', Cnet, 19 August 2021, https://www.cnet.com/tech/computing/virtual-mark-zuckerberg-showed-me-facebooks-new-vr-workplace-solution/

20. Attributed to film director Woody Allen variously as 80 per cent and 90 per cent.

21. Adam Grant, 'Productivity Isn't About Time Management. It's About Attention Management', *New York Times*, 28 March 2019, https://www.nytimes.com/2019/03/28/smarter-living/productivity-isnt-about-time-management-its-about-attention-management.html

22. Daniel Susskind, *A World Without Work: Technology, Automation, and How We Should Respond* (Allen Lane, 2020)

Chapter 4: Shift 4: New Networks

1. Herminia Ibarra, and Mark Lee Hunter, 'How Leaders Create and Use Networks', *Harvard Business Review*, January 2007, https://hbr.org/2007/01/how-leaders-create-and-use-networks; Nicholas A. Christakis, and James H. Fowler, 'Dynamic Spread of Happiness in a Large Social Network: Longitudinal Analysis Over 20 Years in the Framingham Heart Study', *BMJ*, 5 December 2008, https://www.bmj.com/content/337/bmj.a2338; René F. Marineau, 'The Birth and Development of Sociometry: The Work and Legacy of Jacob Moreno (1889–1974)', *Social Psychology Quarterly*, 70 (4): 322–5, December 2007, https://journals.sagepub.com/doi/abs/10.1177/019027250707000402

2. Robert Putnam, *Bowling Alone* (Simon & Schuster, 2000)

3. See Julia Hobsbawm, *Fully Connected: Social Health in an Age of Overload* (Bloomsbury, 2017); also Lynda Gratton, *The Shift: The Future of Work is Already Here* (Collins, 2011)

4. Shawn Achor, 'Do Women's Networking Events Move the Needle on Equality?', *Harvard Business Review*, 13 February 2018, https://hbr.org/2018/02/do-womens-networking-events-move-the-needle-on-equality

5. Mansoor Iqbal, 'LinkedIn Usage and Revenue Statistics (2021)', Business of Apps, 5 July 2021, https://www.businessofapps.com/data/linkedin-statistics/

6. Sarah Perez, 'Report: WhatsApp Has Seen a 40% Increase in Usage Due to Covid-19 Pandemic', TechCrunch, 26 March 2020, https://techcrunch.com/2020/03/26/report-whatsapp-has-seen-a-40-increase-in-usage-due-to-covid-19-pandemic/

7. Frances Cairncross, *The Death of Distance: How the Communications Revolution is Changing Our Lives* (Harvard Business Review Press, 2001)

8. Lin Grensing-Pophal, 'Taking Advantage of a Broader Talent Pool', Society for Human Resource Management, 3 February 2021, https://www.shrm.org/resourcesandtools/hr-topics/talent-acquisition/pages/taking-advantage-of-a-broader-talent-pool.aspx

9. 'Virtual Events Market Size, Share & Trends Analysis Report by Event Type, by Service, by Establishment Size, by End-use, by Application, by Industry Vertical, by Use-case, by Region, and Segment Forecasts, 2021–2028', Grand View Research, July 2021, https://www.grandviewresearch.com/industry-analysis/virtual-events-market

10. Mark S. Granovetter, 'The Strength of Weak Ties', *American Journal of Sociology*, 78 (6): 1360–80, May 1973, https://www.jstor.org/stable/2776392

11. Rob Cross, 'Introduction to Organizational Network Analysis', https://gates.comm.virginia.edu/rlc3w/sna.htm

12. Rob Cross, Kevin Oakes, and Connor Cross, 'Cultivating an Inclusive Culture Through Personal Networks', *MIT Sloan Management Review*, 8 June 2021, https://sloanreview.mit.edu/article/cultivating-an-inclusive-culture-through-personal-networks/

13. Joseph Stiglitz, Amartya Sen, and Jean-Paul Fitoussi, 'Report by the Commission on the Measurement of Economic Performance and Social Progress', 2009, https://ec.europa.eu/eurostat/documents/8131721/8131772/Stiglitz-Sen-Fitoussi-Commission-report.pdf; see this definition of social capital: Will Kenton, 'Social Capital', Investopedia, 24 July 2021, https://www.investopedia.com/terms/s/socialcapital.asp; see also Herminia Ibarra, 'How to Break Through a Career Impasse', 11 October 2013, https://herminiaibarra.com/how-to-break-through-a-career-impasse/

14. Robert L. Cross, Salvatore Parise, and Leigh M. Weiss, 'The Role of Networks in Organizational Change', McKinsey, 1 April 2007, https://www.mckinsey.com/business-functions/organization/our-insights/the-role-of-networks-in-organizational-change

15. Rocío Lorenzo et al., 'How Diverse Leadership Teams Boost Innovation', BCG, 23 January 2018, https://www.bcg.com/en-us/publications/2018/how-diverse-leadership-teams-boost-innovation

16. Sylvia Ann Hewlett, Melinda Marshall, and Laura Sherbin, 'How Diversity Can Drive Innovation', *Harvard Business Review*, December 2013, https://hbr.org/2013/12/how-diversity-can-drive-innovation

17. 'Young Workers: Attitudes to Work, Unions and Society', Report for the European Federation of Public Service Unions (EPSU), May 2019, https://www.epsu.org/sites/default/files/article/files/EN_Young%20workers.pdf

18. Margaret Schweer et al., 'Building a Well-Networked Organization', *MIT Sloan Management Review*, 21 December 2011, https://sloanreview.mit.edu/article/building-a-well-networked-organization/

19. Alicia Kelso, 'Restaurant Industry Expected to Lose \$240B by the End of 2020', Restaurant Dive, 16 June 2020, https://www.restaurantdive.com/news/restaurant-industry-expected-to-lose-240b-by-the-end-of-2020/579857/

20. Interviewed for The Nowhere Office podcast, https://open.spotify.com/show/3SAjjNiMYSNWQTMHazqcRS

21. Brooke Masters, 'Goldman Sachs Complaints Show Long Hours and Covid Don't Mix', *Financial Times*, 23 March 2021, https://www.ft.com/content/19a14cad-b5fc-4fc3-aa5a-ca306af5b831

22. See Ronald S. Burt, *Brokerage & Closure: An Introduction to Social Capital* (Oxford University Press, 2007)

Chapter 5: Shift 5: Marzipan Management

1. Amanda Goodall, 'If You Want to Know Why People Are Reluctant to Be Leaders, Ask Them', *Financial Times*, 6 September 2021, https://www.ft.com/content/4e4f467a-5bef-44a6-bf19-7442f4b78abb

2. For more on the term 'marzipan layer' see https://new_words. en-academic.com/1826/marzipan_layer; see also the jon1.com blog post, 15 January 2010, https://jon1.com/2010/01/15/the-marzipan-layer/; Emiliya Mychasuk, 'Countries Where Women Executives Fare Best', *Financial Times*, 25 September 2009, https://www.ft.com/content/6ad5ff3e-a718-11de-bd14-00144fe-abdco

3. Chris Westfall, 'Leadership Development is a $366 Billion Industry: Here's Why Most Programs Don't Work', *Forbes*, 20 June 2019, https://www.forbes.com/sites/chriswestfall/2019/06/20/leadership-development-why-most-programs-dont-work/?sh=139c593761de

4. Liz Fosslien, and Mollie West Duffy, *No Hard Feelings: Emotions at Work (and How They Help Us Succeed)* (Penguin Business, 2019)

5. See Barbara Kellerman, *Bad Leadership: What It Is, How It Happens, Why It Matters* (Harvard Business Review Press, 2004)

6. Olaf Storbeck, 'Wirecard: A Record of Deception, Disarray and Mismanagement', *Financial Times*, 24 June 2021, https://www.ft.com/content/15bb36e7-54dc-463a-a6d5-70fc38a11c81

7. See Juliet Hassard et al., 'The Cost of Work-Related Stress to Society: A Systematic Review', http://irep.ntu.ac.uk/id/eprint/30155/1/PubSub7909_Hassard.pdf; also Jean-Pierre Brun, 'Work-Related Stress: Scientific Evidence-Base of Risk Factors, Prevention And Costs', WHO, 13 March 2007, https://www.who.int/occupational_health/topics/brunpreso307.pdf; see also Gallup State of the Global Workplace report, 'A Global Pandemic and Its Impact on Global Engagement, Stress and the Workforce', Gallup, https://www.gallup.com/workplace/349484/state-of-the-global-workplace.aspx; and John M. Ivancevich, Michael T. Matteson, and Edward P. Richards, 'Who's Liable for Stress on the Job?', *Harvard Business Review*, March 1985, https://hbr.org/1985/03/whos-liable-for-stress-on-the-job

8. World Health Organisation, 'Occupational Health: Stress at

the Workplace', 19 October 2020, https://www.who.int/news-room/q-a-detail/ccupational-health-stress-at-the-workplace

9. 2021 Edelman Trust Barometer, https://www.edelman.com/trust/2021-trust-barometer

10. 'Autonomy in the Workplace Has Positive Effects on Well-Being and Job Satisfaction, Study Finds', University of Birmingham, 24 April 2017, https://www.birmingham.ac.uk/news/latest/2017/04/autonomy-workplace.aspx

11. See 'The Great Resignation: Why People Are Leaving Their Jobs in Growing Numbers', NPR, 22 October 2021, https://www.npr.org/2021/10/22/1048332481/the-great-resignation-why-people-are-leaving-their-jobs-in-growing-numbers; EY Study, 'More Than Half of Employees Globally Would Quit Their Jobs if Not Provided Post-Pandemic Flexibility', 21 May 2021, https://www.ey.com/en_ro/news/2021/05/ey-study--more-than-half-of-employees-globally-would-quit-their-

12. Julia Hobsbawm, 'Lessons in Simplicity Strategy', *Strategy + Business*, 29 April 2021, https://www.strategy-business.com/article/Lessons-in-simplicity-strategy

13. Ibid., but see also Julia Hobsbawm, *The Simplicity Principle: Six Steps Towards Clarity in a Complex World* (Kogan Page, 2020) and Johnjoe McFadden, *Life is Simple: How Occam's Razor Set Science Free and Unlocked the Universe* (Basic Books, 2021)

14. 'Mindfulness Meditation Apps Market Share, Size, Trends, Industry Analysis Report, by Operating System (Android, iOS, Others); by Service Type (Paid-in App Purchases, Free); by Age Group (6–12 Years Old, 13–18 Years Old, and 19 Above); by Regions; Segment Forecast, 2020–2027', Polaris Market Research, October 2020, https://www.polarismarketresearch.com/industry-analysis/mindfulness-meditation-apps-market

15. Dashun Wang, and James A. Evans, 'Research: When Small Teams Are Better Than Big Ones', *Harvard Business Review*, 21 February 2019, https://hbr.org/2019/02/research-when-small-teams-are-better-than-big-ones

16. Susan M. Heathfield, 'Reasons Why Employees Hate HR',

16 February 2021, https://www.thebalancecareers.com/reasons-why-employees-hate-hr-1917590

17. QLK Team, 'Evolution of Human Resources Management', Quick Leonard Kieffer, 23 February 2017, https://www.qlksearch.com/blog/evolution-of-human-resources

18. According to this market report, 'Core HR Software Market by Software (Learning Management, Payroll and Compensation Management), Service, Deployment Type (On-Premises and Cloud), Organization Size (SMEs and Large Enterprises), Vertical, and Region – Global Forecast to 2022', Markets and Marketing, May 2017, https://www.marketsandmarkets.com/Market-Reports/core-human-resource-hr-software-market-81186018.html

19. Elizabeth Uviebiné, 'Annual Performance Reviews Do a Disservice to Workers and Firms', *Financial Times*, 29 November 2019, https://www.ft.com/content/f579e8c8-0f8e-11ea-a7e6-62bf4f9e548a; see also Elizabeth Uviebiné, *The Reset: Ideas to Change How We Work and Live* (Hodder Studio, 2021)

20. Reggie Van Lee, Chief Transformation Officer at Carlyle Group, Bloomberg Work Summit, spring 2021

21. Interviewed for The Nowhere Office podcast, https://open.spotify.com/show/3SAjjNiMYSNWQTMHazqcRS

Chapter 6: Shift 6: Social Health and Well-being

1. WHO definition of health, 1948: 'A state of complete physical, mental and social well-being and not merely the absence of disease or infirmity', https://www.who.int/about/governance/constitution

2. 'Corporate Wellness Market Size, Share & Trends Analysis Report by Service (Health Risk Assessment, Fitness), by End-use, by Category, by Delivery Model (Onsite, Offsite), by Region, and Segment Forecasts, 2021–2028', Grand View

Research, March 2021, https://www.grandviewresearch.com/industry-analysis/corporate-wellness-market

3. 'Financial Costs of Job Stress', UMass Lowell, https://www.uml.edu/research/cph-new/worker/stress-at-work/financial-costs.aspx; John Daly, 'Stress Accounts for 60% of All Lost Days in the Workplace', *Irish Examiner*, 9 October 2015, https://www.irishexaminer.com/business/arid-20358497.html; see EndStress EU for data and perspectives on stress, https://endstress.eu

4. Zoe Wickens, '26% of Millennials Took Time Off Work Due to Stress', Employee Benefits, 17 June 2021, https://employee-benefits.co.uk/26-millennials-took-time-off-work-stress/; '2021 Retention Report: The Covid Edition', Work Institute, https://info.workinstitute.com/hubfs/Retention%20Reports/2021%20Retention%20Report/Work%20Institutes%202021%20Retention%20Report.pdf

5. '2021 Work Trend Index: Annual Report, The Next Great Disruption Is Hybrid Work – Are We Ready?', 22 March 2021, https://ms-worklab.azureedge.net/files/reports/hybridWork/pdf/2021_Microsoft_WTI_Report_March.pdf.

6. 'Number of Freelance Workers in the United States from 2014 to 2020', Statista, September 2020, https://www.statista.com/statistics/685468/amount-of-people-freelancing-us/; '25 Interesting UK Freelancer Stats & Trends (2021)', YourMoney, 5 May 2021, https://yourmoney.lumio-app.com/uk-freelancer-statistics-trends/

7. 'Burn-Out an "Occupational Phenomenon": International Classification of Diseases', World Health Organisation, 28 May 2019, https://www.who.int/news/item/28-05-2019-burn-out-an-occupational-phenomenon-international-classification-of-diseases

8. Ibid.

9. Michael Rucker, 'The Interesting History of Workplace Wellness', Michaelrucker.com, 20 May 2016, https://michaelrucker.com/well-being/the-history-of-workplace-wellness/. For a good all-round history of workplace well-

being and on 'Healthy People 2000' see National Center for Health Statistics, https://www.cdc.gov/nchs/healthy_people/hp2000.htm; see also Jeffrey Pfeffer, 'The Overlooked Essentials of Employee Well-Being', McKinsey, 11 September 2018, https://www.mckinsey.com/business-functions/organization/our-insights/the-overlooked-essentials-of-employee-well-being

10. Joseph Stiglitz, Amartya Sen, and Jean-Paul Fitoussi, 'Report by the Commission on the Measurement of Economic Performance and Social Progress', 2009, https://ec.europa.eu/eurostat/documents/8131721/8131772/Stiglitz-Sen-Fitoussi-Commission-report.pdf

11. Julia Hobsbawm, 'It's Time For Social Health', Thrive Global, 18 June 2018, https://thriveglobal.com/stories/it-s-time-for-social-health/

12. Benjamin M. Artz, Amanda H. Goodall, and Andrew J. Oswald, 'Boss Competence and Worker Well-Being', *International Labour Review*, 70 (2): 419–50, March 2017, http://www.amandagoodall.com/BossCompetenceILLRPub.pdf; Amanda Goodall, 'If You Want to Know Why People Are Reluctant to Be Leaders, Ask Them', *Financial Times*, 6 September 2021, https://www.ft.com/content/4e4f467a-5bef-44a6-bf19-7442f4b78abb; Tera Allas, David Chinn, Pal Erik Sjatil, and Whitney Zimmerman, 'Well-Being in Europe: Addressing the High Cost Of Covid-19 on Life Satisfaction', McKinsey, 9 June 2020, https://www.mckinsey.com/featured-insights/europe/well-being-in-europe-addressing-the-high-cost-of-covid-19-on-life-satisfaction

13. Kate Conger, 'Culture Change and Conflict at Twitter', *New York Times*, 16 August 2021, https://www.nytimes.com/2021/08/16/technology/twitter-culture-change-conflict.html

14. Caitlin Powell, 'Quarter of Employees Have Been Bullied at Work, Survey Finds', *People Management*, 2 June 2021, https://www.peoplemanagement.co.uk/news/articles/quarter-of-employees-have-been-bullied-at-work

15. 'Right to Disconnect: Ensuring a Fair Work-Life Balance',

Prospect, 4 November 2020, https://prospect.org.uk/news/right-to-disconnect/

16. 'One Year Later, a New Wave of Pandemic Health Concerns', American Psychological Association, 11 March 2021, https://www.apa.org/news/press/releases/stress/2021/one-year-pandemic-stress

17. 'Loneliness and the Workplace – 2020 U.S. Report', Cigna, https://www.cigna.com/static/www-cigna-com/docs/about-us/newsroom/studies-and-reports/combatting-loneliness/cigna-2020-loneliness-infographic.pdf

Reinventions

1. Chris Kane, *Where is My Office? Reimagining the Workplace for the 21st Century* (Bloomsbury, 2020)

2. John Arlidge, 'Interview: Mark Thompson on the Tonic That Revived the *New York Times*', *The Times*, 30 August 2020, https://www.thetimes.co.uk/article/interview-mark-thompson-on-the-tonic-that-revived-the-new-york-times-9qskbkq25

3. 'The End of the Office', Seth's Blog, 6 August 2021, https://seths.blog/2021/08/the-end-of-the-office/

4. Elaine Mullan, 'The First AI Machine Will Join a Corporate Board of Directors by 2026 – Really?', LinkedIn, 20 October 2017, https://www.linkedin.com/pulse/first-ai-machine-join-corporate-board-directors-2026-elaine-mullan/

5. See https://www.worldxo.org/

6. Paul Kelly and Sian Griffiths, *Body Clocks: The Biology of Time for Sleep, Education and Work* (John Catt, 2018)

7. See Andrew Pakes, 'The Right to Disconnect', Institute for the Future of Work, 16 April 2021, https://www.ifow.org/news-articles/the-right-to-disconnect

8. See 'Arup Embraces Seven-Day Work Week With Flexible Hours', Consultancy.uk, 21 May 2021, https://www.consultancy.uk/news/27991/arup-embraces-seven-day-work-week-with-

flexible-hours; and Karen Thomson, 'Work-Life Shift: Making Flexible Working the Norm', Fujitsu UK, 12 February 2021, https://blog.uk.fujitsu.com/responsible-business/work-life-shift-making-flexible-working-the-norm/#.YYFtgp7P2Uk

9. Diane Coyle, 'A Time-Based Approach to Measuring Economic Welfare', Economic Statistics Centre of Excellence, 22 January 2019, https://www.escoe.ac.uk/a-time-based-approach-to-measuring-economic-welfare/

10. See Glassdoor, a leader on insights into jobs and companies, https://www.glassdoor.com/about-us/

11. H. Tajfel, and J. C. Turner, 'An Integrative Theory of Intergroup Conflict', in W. G. Austin, and S. Worchel (eds), *The Social Psychology of Intergroup Relations*, pp. 33–7 (Brooks/Cole, 1979)

12. 'KISS (Keep it Simple, Stupid) – A Design Principle', Interaction Design Foundation, https://www.interaction-design.org/literature/article/kiss-keep-it-simple-stupid-a-design-principle

13. 'Apparently, It's the Next Big Thing: What is the Metaverse?', BBC News, 18 October 2021, https://www.bbc.co.uk/news/technology-58749529

Further Reading

The following resources relate particularly to these individual chapters but can, of course, apply across the subject matter of the book as whole.

Introduction

Baker, Nicholson, *The Mezzanine* (Granta, 2011)
Turkle, Sherry, *Alone Together: Why We Expect More from Technology and Less from Each Other* (Basic Books, 2011)

Chapter 1: Shift 1: Placeless, Timeless

Flaherty, Michael G., *The Textures of Time: Agency and Temporal Experience* (Temple University Press, 2011)
Garfield, Simon, *Timekeepers: How the World Became Obsessed with Time* (Canongate, 2016)
Gratton, Lynda, and Andrew Scott, *The 100-Year Life: Living and Working in an Age of Longevity* (Bloomsbury, 2020)
Gregg, Melissa, *Work's Intimacy* (Polity Press, 2011)
——, *Counterproductive: Time Management in the Knowledge Economy* (Duke University Press, 2018)
Hochschild, Arlie Russell, *The Second Shift: Working Families and the Revolution at Home* (Penguin, 2012 [1989])

——, *The Time Bind: When Work Becomes Home and Home Becomes Work* (Holt Paperbacks, 2001 [1997])

Hunnicutt, Benjamin Kline, *Kellogg's Six-Hour Day* (Temple University Press, 1996)

Johnson, Elsbeth, *Step Up, Step Back: How to Really Deliver Strategic Change in Your Organisation* (Bloomsbury Business, 2020)

Kane, Chris, *Where is My Office? Reimagining the Workplace for the 21st Century* (Bloomsbury, 2020)

McGilchrist, Iain, *Ways of Attending: How Our Divided Brain Constructs the World* (Routledge, 2019)

Massey, Doreen, 'A Global Sense of Place', *Marxism Today*, June 1991, http://banmarchive.org.uk/collections/mt/pdf/91_06_24.pdf

Russell, Bertrand, 'In Praise of Idleness', *In Praise of Idleness and Other Stories* (Routledge, 2004 [1935])

Saval, Nikil, *Cubed: The Secret History of the Workplace* (Doubleday, 2014)

Saxenian, Annalee: *Regional Advantage: Culture and Competition in Silicon Valley and Route 128* (Harvard University Press, 1996)

Scarry, Richard, *What Do People Do All Day?* (HarperCollins, 2015 [1968])

Smil, Vaclav, *Growth: From Microorganisms to Megacities* (MIT Press, 2020)

Suzman, James, *Work: A History of How We Spend Our Time* (Bloomsbury, 2021)

Usher, Neil, *The Elemental Workplace* (LID Publishing, 2018)

Wajcman, Judy, *Pressed for Time: The Acceleration of Life in Digital Capitalism* (University of Chicago Press, 2015)

Wallman, James, *Time and How to Spend It: The 7 Rules for Richer, Happier Days* (W. H. Allen, 2019)

Chapter 2: Shift 2: Worker Beings

Armstrong, Leah, and Felice McDowell (eds), *Fashioning Professionals: Identity and Representation at Work in the Creative Industries* (Bloomsbury Academic, 2018)

Auerbach, Annie, *Flex: Reinventing Work for a Smarter, Happier Life* (HQ, 2021)

D'Souza, Steven, and Diana Renner, *Not Knowing: The Art of Turning Uncertainty into Opportunity* (LID Publishing, 2014)

Duffy, Bobby, *Generations: Does When You're Born Shape Who You Are?* (Atlantic, 2021)

Ferriss, Tim, *The 4-Hour Work Week* (Vermilion, 2011)

Handy, Charles, *The Empty Raincoat: Making Sense of the Future* (Random House Business, 1995)

——, *Myself, and Other Important Matters* (Arrow Books, 2007)

Hougaard, Rasmus, with Jacqueline Carter, and Gillian Coutts, *One Second Ahead: Enhance Your Performance at Work with Mindfulness* (Palgrave Macmillan, 2015)

Ibarra, Herminia, *Working Identity: Unconventional Strategies for Reinventing Your Career* (Harvard Business Review Press, 2004)

Lucassen, Jan, *The Story of Work: A New History of Humankind* (Yale University Press, 2021)

Morrissey, Helena, *Style and Substance: A Guide for Women Who Want to Win at Work* (Piatkus, 2021)

Moshfegh, Ottessa, *My Year of Rest and Relaxation* (Vintage, 2019)

Pew Research Center, 'On the Cusp of Adulthood and Facing an Uncertain Future: What We Know About Gen Z So Far', https://www.pewresearch.org/social-trends/2020/05/14/on-the-cusp-of-adulthood-and-facing-an-uncertain-future-what-we-know-about-gen-z-so-far-2/

Rosenthal, Caitlin, *Accounting for Slavery: Masters and Management* (Harvard University Press, 2019)

Weisberger, Lauren, *The Devil Wears Prada* (Doubleday, 2003)

Chapter 3: Shift 3: The Productivity Puzzle

Cohen, Josh, *Not Working: Why We Have to Stop* (Granta, 2018)

Crawford, Matthew B., *Shop Class as Soulcraft: An Inquiry into the Value of Work* (Penguin Press, 2009)

Frayne, David, *The Refusal of Work: The Theory and Practice of Resistance to Work* (Zed, 2015)

Graeber, David, *Bullshit Jobs: The Rise of Pointless Work, and What We Can Do About It* (Allen Lane, 2018)

Horowitz, Sara, *Mutualism: Building the Next Economy from the Ground Up* (Random House, 2021)

Jaffe, Sarah, *Work Won't Love You Back: How Devotion to Our Jobs Keeps Us Exploited, Exhausted and Alone* (Hurst, 2021)

Jeevan, Sharath, *Intrinsic: A Manifesto to Reignite Our Inner Drive* (Endeavour, 2021)

Kanter, Rosabeth Moss, *Commitment and Community: Communes and Utopias in Sociological Perspective* (Harvard University Press, 1972)

Mayer, Colin, *Firm Commitment: Why the Corporation is Failing Us and How to Restore Trust in It* (Oxford University Press, 2013)

Newport, Cal, *Deep Work: Rules For Focused Success in a Distracted World* (Piatkus, 2016)

Russell, Bertrand, 'In Praise of Idleness', *In Praise of Idleness* (Routledge Classics, 2004 [1935])

Shafik, Minouche, *What We Owe Each Other: A New Social Contract* (Bodley Head, 2021)

Sinclair, Upton, *The Jungle* (Penguin, 2002 [1906])

Soojung-Kim Pang, Alex, *Rest: Why You Get More Done When You Work Less* (Penguin Life, 2017)

Wooldridge, Adrian, *The Aristocracy of Talent: How Meritocracy Made the Modern World* (Allen Lane, 2021)

Chapter 4: Shift 4: New Networks

Baker, Wayne, *Networking Smart: How to Build Relationships for Personal and Organizational Success* (McGraw-Hill, 1994)

Burt, Ronald S., *Brokerage and Closure: An Introduction to Social Capital* (Oxford University Press, 2007)

Cairncross, Frances, *The Death of Distance: How the Communications*

Revolution is Changing Our Lives (Harvard Business Review Press, 2001)

Christakis, Nicholas A., and James H. Fowler, *Connected: The Surprising Power of Our Social Networks and How They Shape Our Lives* (Little, Brown, 2009)

Easley, David, and Jon Kleinberg, *Networks, Crowds and Markets: Reasoning About a Highly Connected World* (Cambridge University Press, 2010)

Ferguson, Niall, *The Square and the Tower: Networks, Hierarchies and the Struggle for Global Power* (Penguin, 2018)

Gratton, Lynda, *The Shift: The Future of Work is Already Here* (Collins, 2011)

Hertz, Noreena, *The Lonely Century: Coming Together in a World That's Pulling Apart* (Sceptre, 2020)

Hobsbawm, Julia, *Fully Connected: Social Health in an Age of Overload* (Bloomsbury, 2017)

Margonelli, Lisa, *Underbug: An Obsessive Tale of Termites and Technology* (Scientific American/Farrar, Straus and Giroux, 2018)

Pinker, Susan, *The Village Effect: Why Face-to-Face Contact Matters* (Atlantic, 2014)

Putnam, Robert, *Bowling Alone* (Simon & Schuster, 2000)

Ryckman, Pamela, *Stiletto Network: Inside the Women's Power Circles That Are Changing the Face of Business* (Amacom, 2013)

Sandberg, Sheryl, *Lean In: Women, Work and the Will to Lead* (W. H. Allen, 2013)

Unerman, Sue, Kathryn Jacobs, and Mark Edwards, *Belonging: The Key to Transforming and Maintaining Diversity, Inclusion and Equality at Work* (Bloomsbury Business, 2020)

Chapter 5: Shift 5: Marzipan Management

Ashcroft, Paul, and Garrick Jones, *Alive: Digital Humans and their Organizations* (Novaro Publishing, 2018)

Daisley, Bruce, *The Joy of Work: 30 Ways to Fix Your Work Culture and Fall in Love with Your Job Again* (Random House Business, 2019)

Hamel, Gary, and Michele Zanini, *Humanocracy: Creating Organizations as Amazing as the People Inside Them* (Harvard Business Review Press, 2020)

Handy, Charles, *Understanding Organizations* (Penguin, 1993)

Hobsbawm, Julia, *The Simplicity Principle: Six Steps Towards Clarity in a Complex World* (Kogan Page, 2020)

Ibarra, Herminia, *Think Like a Leader, Act Like a Leader* (Harvard Business Review Press, 2015)

Johnson, Elsbeth, *Step Up, Step Back: How to Really Deliver Strategic Change in Your Organisation* (Bloomsbury Business, 2020)

Kellerman, Barbara, *Bad Leadership: What It Is, How It Happens, Why It Matters* (Harvard Business Review Press, 2004)

——, *The End of Leadership* (Harper Business, 2012)

Moyo, Dambisa, *How Boards Work and How They Can Work Better in a Chaotic World* (Bridge Street Press, 2021)

Norman, Donald A., *Living with Complexity* (MIT Press, 2016)

Rumelt, Richard, *Good Strategy, Bad Strategy: The Difference and Why it Matters* (Profile, 2017 [2011])

Stern, Stefan, and Cary Cooper, *Myths of Management: What People Get Wrong About Being the Boss (Business Myths)* (Kogan Page, 2017)

Chapter 6: Shift 6: Social Health and Well-being

Aitsi-Selmi, Amina, *The Success Trap: Why Good People Stay in Jobs They Don't Like and How to Break Free* (Kogan Page, 2020)

Beckett, Samuel, *Happy Days* (Faber, 2010 [1961])

Cooper, Cary, and Ian Hesketh, *Wellbeing at Work: How to Design, Implement and Evaluate an Effective Strategy* (Kogan Page, 2019)

Draper, Derek, *Create Space: How to Manage Time and Find Focus, Productivity and Success* (Profile, 2018)

Kahneman, Daniel, Olivier Sibony, and Cass Sunstein, *Noise: A Flaw in Human Judgement* (William Collins, 2021)

Laloux, Frederic, *Reinventing Organizations: A Guide to Creating Organizations Inspired by the Next Stage of Human Consciousness* (Nelson Parker, 2014)

Lyons, Dan, *Lab Rats: Why Modern Work Makes People Miserable* (Atlantic, 2019)

Newport, Cal, *Digital Minimalism: Living Better with Less Technology* (Portfolio/Penguin, 2019)

Orbach, Susie, *What's Really Going on Here: Making Sense of our Emotional Lives* (Virago, 1994)

Russell, Bertrand, *The Conquest of Happiness* (Routledge Classics, 2006 [1930])

Selye, Hans, *The Stress of Life* (McGraw Hill, 1956)

Turkle, Sherry, *Alone Together: Why We Expect More from Technology and Less from Each Other* (Basic Books, 2011)

Workforce Institute at Kronos, *Being Present: A Practical Guide for Transforming the Employee Experience of your Frontline Workforce* (Kronos, 2019)

Reinventions

Kelly, Paul, and Sian Griffiths, *Body Clocks: The Biology of Time for Sleep, Education and Work* (John Catt, 2018)

Note on Further Reading

I list below some of the books (fiction and non-fiction) and datasets to help your thinking as a whole. By no means a complete bibliography, this a starting point for further reading. You can also download my podcast The Nowhere Office on all podcast platforms, and sign up to newsletters from www.juliahobsbawm.com.

Arendt, Hannah, *The Human Condition* (University of Chicago Press, 1998 [1958])

Avent, Ryan, *The Wealth of Humans* (Allen Lane, 2016)

British Academy, Future of the Corporation, https://www. thebritishacademy.ac.uk/programmes/future-of-the-corporation/

Brynjolfsson, Eric, and Andrew McAfee, *The Second Machine Age: Work, Progress, and Prosperity in a Time of Brilliant Technologies* (W. W. Norton & Co., 2014)

Chapman, Tim, *Why Workplace: A Leader's Guide to Rebuilding the Post-Pandemic Workplace* (Leesman, 2021)

Cséfalvay, Zoltán, *TECHtonic Shifts* (Kairosz Kiadó, 2017)

Cushman & Wakefield Workplace Insights, https://www.cushman-wakefield.com/en/insights/covid-19/the-future-of-workplace

d'Ancona, Matthew, *Identity, Ignorance, Innovation: Why the Old Politics is Useless – and What to Do About It* (Hodder & Stoughton, 2021)

Ferris, Joshua, *Then We Came to the End* (Penguin, 2008)

Fosslien, Liz, and Mollie West Duffy, *No Hard Feelings: Emotions at Work (and How They Help Us Succeed)* (Penguin Business, 2019)

Galbraith, Robert, *The Cuckoo's Calling* (Sphere, 2014)

Gallup Workplace portal, https://www.gallup.com/topic/workplace.aspx

Gratton, Lynda, and Andrew Scott, *The 100-Year Life: Living and Working in an Age of Longevity* (Bloomsbury Business, 2017)

Hazzard, Shirley, *Collected Stories* (Virago, 2020)

Hobsbawm, Julia, *The Nowhere Office* (Demos, 2021), https://demos.co.uk/project/the-nowhere-office/

Hochschild, Arlie Russell, *The Outsourced Self: What Happens When We Pay Others to Live Our Lives for Us* (Metropolitan Books, 2012)

Howkins, John, *Invisible Work: The Future of the Office is in Your Head* (September Publishing, 2021)

International Labour Organisation (ILO) https://www.ilo.org/global/lang--en/index.htm

Ipsos's workplace polling, https://www.ipsos.com/en/search?search=workplace

Leesman Index, https://www.leesmanindex.com/

McEwan, Ian, *Machines Like Me* (Vintage, 2020)

McKinsey, Future of Work portal, https://www.mckinsey.com/featured-insights/future-of-work

Mayhew, Henry, *London Labour and the London Poor: A Selected Edition* (Oxford University Press, 2010)

Melville, Herman, *Bartleby, the Scrivener: A Story of Wall Street* (SMK, 2012 [1853])

Microsoft Work Insights portal, https://workplaceinsights.microsoft.com/

Murdoch, Iris, *A Word Child* (Vintage Classics, 2008 [1975])

OECD Future of Work portal, https://www.oecd.org/future-of-work/reports-and-data/

Office for National Statistics, Coronavirus (Covid-19) latest insights, https://www.ons.gov.uk/peoplepopulationandcommunity/healthandsocialcare/conditionsanddiseases/articles/coronaviruscovid19/latestinsights

Roberts, Simon, *The Power of Not Thinking: How Our Bodies Learn and Why We Should Trust Them* (Blink Publishing, 2020)

Robson, David, *The Intelligence Trap: Why Smart People Do Stupid Things and How to Make Wiser Decisions* (Hodder & Stoughton, 2019)

Rushkoff, Douglas, *Team Human* (Norton, 2019)

Sandburg, Carl, *Chicago Poems* (Dover, 1994 [1916])

Spark, Muriel, *A Far Cry from Kensington* (Polygon, 2017 [1988])

Susskind, Daniel, *A World Without Work: Technology, Automation and How We Should Respond* (Allen Lane, 2020)

Terkel, Studs, *Working: People Talk About What They Do All Day and How They Feel About What They Do* (New Press, 1974)

Tett, Gillian, *Anthro-Vision: How Anthropology Can Explain Business and Life* (Penguin, 2021)

Tomasello, Michael, *The Cultural Origins of Human Cognition* (Harvard University Press, 1999)

Uviebiné, Elizabeth, *The Reset: Ideas to Change How We Work and Live* (Hodder Studio, 2021)

West, Geoffrey, *Scale: The Universal Laws of Life and Death in Organisms, Cities and Companies* (Weidenfeld & Nicolson, 2017)

Wolf, Martin, *The Shifts and the Shocks: What We've Learned – and Have Still to Learn – from the Financial Crisis* (Allen Lane, 2014)

World Bank, *World Development Report 2019: The Changing Nature of Work*, https://www.worldbank.org/en/publication/wdr2019

World Economic Forum (WEF) Preparing for the Future of Work portal, https://www.weforum.org/projects/future-of-work

World Experience Organization, https://www.worldxo.org/

Index

Julia Hobsbawm is an entrepreneur, writer, and consultant who addresses the challenges of the hyper connected age, in particular remedies of what she has called "social health" for organizations.

She is chair of The Workshift Commission and is founder and chair of the content and connection business Editorial Intelligence. Her bestselling book *The Simplicity Principle: Six Steps Towards Clarity in a Complex World* was published in 2020.

Awarded an OBE for services to business, her articles are amongst the most downloaded on the Strategy + Business site and she is an adviser to the British Academy's Future of the Corporation project.

PublicAffairs is a publishing house founded in 1997. It is a tribute to the standards, values, and flair of three persons who have served as mentors to countless reporters, writers, editors, and book people of all kinds, including me.

I. F. Stone, proprietor of *I. F. Stone's Weekly*, combined a commitment to the First Amendment with entrepreneurial zeal and reporting skill and became one of the great independent journalists in American history. At the age of eighty, Izzy published *The Trial of Socrates*, which was a national bestseller. He wrote the book after he taught himself ancient Greek.

Benjamin C. Bradlee was for nearly thirty years the charismatic editorial leader of *The Washington Post*. It was Ben who gave the *Post* the range and courage to pursue such historic issues as Watergate. He supported his reporters with a tenacity that made them fearless and it is no accident that so many became authors of influential, best-selling books.

Robert L. Bernstein, the chief executive of Random House for more than a quarter century, guided one of the nation's premier publishing houses. Bob was personally responsible for many books of political dissent and argument that challenged tyranny around the globe. He is also the founder and longtime chair of Human Rights Watch, one of the most respected human rights organizations in the world.

·   ·   ·

For fifty years, the banner of Public Affairs Press was carried by its owner Morris B. Schnapper, who published Gandhi, Nasser, Toynbee, Truman, and about 1,500 other authors. In 1983, Schnapper was described by *The Washington Post* as "a redoubtable gadfly." His legacy will endure in the books to come.

Peter Osnos, *Founder*